SHE INSPIRED

A COLLECTION OF INSPIRATIONAL STORIES FROM AROUND THE WORLD

D.A. BATROWNY

Copyright © 2023 by Buffdon Publishing.
All Rights Reserved.

No part of this publication may be reproduced, distributed, or transmitted in any form or by any means, including photocopying, recording, or other electronic or mechanical methods, or by any information storage and retrieval system without the prior written permission of the publisher, except in the case of very brief quotations embodied in critical reviews and certain other non-commercial uses permitted by copyright law.

The stories described within this book are each writer's personal thoughts. The author does not assume and hereby disclaims any liability to any party for any loss, damage, or disruption caused by errors or omissions, whether such errors or omissions result from accident, negligence, or any other cause.

The information contained in this book is intended to be for entertainment purposes only and not for diagnosis or treatment and should not be used as a substitute for any professional services. The author and publisher are in no way liable for any misuse of the material.

First edition: 2023

DEDICATION

This book is dedicated to the parents around the world who inspire and motivate others by not giving up on their dreams.

You continue to inspire us every day!

ACKNOWLEDGEMENTS

From the very depths of my soul, I would like to thank everyone who contributed their story and supported the creation of this book. It would not exist without you. I was amazed by the offers to share so many wonderful stories from around the world. I will forever be grateful.

Contents

PREFACE 1
WHY I WROTE THIS BOOK 3
INTRODUCTION 5
    Life Is What You Make It 7
INSPIRING STORIES FROM THE HEART 9
    Miles of Memories 11
    From Homeless to Home 15
    Grandmother's Dream 17
    A Birthday to Remember 21
    Sweet Intentions 23
    My Mother's Touch 25
    Negative to Positive 27
    Perseverance and Strength 29
    Never Too Late 31
    Loving and Strong 33
    I've Got This 35
    Be Yourself 37
    Let's Empower Our Kids 41
    I Really Can 45
    They Watch Us Every Day 49
    Balance and Self-Care 51
    Passing It Down 55
    This Is My Dream 57
    From This Moment On 59

Life is Short 61
Journey from Low Confidence to Success 63
All the Love in Her Heart 65
A Resilient Spirit 69
Moving Forward Together 71
No Longer Weighted Down 75
Meeting to Remember 79
Never Give Up 83
Reborn 87
A Life Worth Watching 91
Lessons from My Mother 93
The Art of Silence 95
All Shall Be Well 97
In Her I Find Strength 101

FINAL THOUGHTS 105
ABOUT THE AUTHOR 109

PREFACE

After writing *The Power of Moms with Dreams*, I started to hear readers' stories about the many ways that the information in the book was helpful to them as they lived their daily lives and followed their dreams. I discovered such a variety of stories of parents who chased their personal dreams while raising children, and the positive impact this also had on their children, whether intended or not. As I reached out, I discovered many other parents and children who were impacted by their own parents' positive choices. I knew these inspiring stories had to be shared.

Some of the stories include simple observations that a child made while casually observing their mother, which then made a positive impact on the child, and some of the stories include life-changing decisions that made an impact far into the future, when the child became an adult. Many of the stories show how parents' actions influence a child's life, even when they may not be aware that they are. They also show that even when parents are faced with life-changing obstacles that feel insurmountable in the moment, there may be a great lesson that the child is taking away from that very situation that may help them immediately or later in life.

Many agree that being a parent is difficult at times. It can be hard enough to make it through the day-to-day routines, even without attempting to achieve your own personal dreams. There can be obstacles, fear, guilt, resentment, frustration, exhaustion, as well as all the wonderful moments sprinkled throughout.

With over 20 years working with mothers and children, which included work as a longitudinal research team member, working one-on-one with parents and their children, and as a director of developmental programs for children and families, I witnessed the truth about the well-known saying, "Children learn from what you do, not what you say." The stories in this book will also reveal how parents and caregivers are modeling to children every day, through direct experiences and a child's observations. Of course, I do not believe there is such a thing as a perfect parent. We all do the best we can and learn along the way. You will get a glimpse of this as you read the inspiring stories in this book, and you will also discover how even the smallest positive actions can leave a lasting impression on those we love.

WHY I WROTE THIS BOOK

I wrote this book for many reasons, including my love of writing, my desire to inspire others, and my wish to spread the love of reading to others. But most of all, I wrote this book, along with all the wonderful authors who shared a piece of their own lives, to show the infinite number of ways that a mother, parent, caregiver, and teacher can inspire a child, even when they may not know they are doing so. Children are there, silently watching.

One message taken from my book, *The Power of Moms with Dreams*, is that talking with our children is important, but the message conveyed through modeling to our children, whether we know we are doing it or not, can make an impact for life.

The stories included in this book will convey this very message. My hope is that they inspire you, motivate you, and convey to you the message that as easy or as difficult life gets, don't give up because your children are watching and their lives may be changed now and in the future by the actions you take.

I first planned to write this book to inspire moms as a follow up to my book, *The Power of Moms with Dreams*, which includes easy steps moms can use to follow their dreams while successfully modeling the same simple concepts to their children, but a very insightful friend of mine explained that this book can inspire not only moms, but dads, adult children and everyone who reads it. I quickly discovered evidence of this as I began collecting the stories for this book. Several authors explained that although they were not moms themselves, they had wonderful examples of how their own parent's or grandparent's actions created lasting inspiration within them. They shared that the lessons they learned from those actions were instrumental in positively impacting their lives and decisions throughout life. So, whether you are a parent or not, you are a child of a parent and most likely were raised by a parent or parent figure who impacted your life in some manner. As you read the stories in this book, you will discover the multitude of ways a child's life can be positively changed by the actions and love of another.

I want to thank my dear friend John, my mastermind group friends, and especially the authors of the heartfelt stories for broadening my approach and getting this book into the hands of everyone looking for beautiful lessons of love.

INTRODUCTION

I think the best place to start is with my own personal story that I also shared in my book, *The Power of Moms with Dreams*. This story was instrumental in demonstrating to me how a life can be permanently impacted by those who care for that life and how the positive way a parent or caregiver approaches their own life can create long lasting lessons that can be attributed to the future success habits of the child.

Life Is What You Make It

D.B., New York, USA

I didn't think my childhood was any different than that of many of my friends. I played outside, went on yearly vacations, and attended Sunday school. One day, I was talking to a friend who was telling me about an acquaintance of hers who told her that she had experienced a "terrible childhood." This friend was blaming her present life situation on her childhood. As I listened to my friend speak, I was stunned. Many of the "terrible" things her friend was saying that had happened during her childhood had also happened to me, yet I never viewed my life as "terrible." I always believed I had a great childhood. I thought about this for days. I wondered why two people could react so differently to such similar situations.

Let me tell you a bit about my childhood. When I was seven years old, my father received a severe traumatic brain injury in an automobile accident and was in a coma for many months. At that time, the doctors said that if he lived, the best place for him was in a nursing home because they felt he would have to learn all his skills over again and would never be independent. After much convincing and promising, my mother finally was able to get the doctors to agree to let my father come home. She spent many hours teaching my father simple activities like using eating utensils and walking. There were emergency calls when he would experience a seizure, and for quite a while after his injury, we had to keep the doors locked so he would not wander out of the house on his own.

So, let me tell you why I always felt that I had a happy childhood. My mother's actions set the tone. My mother was positive. She did not complain about our circumstances. She continued to keep positive about life and always viewed the bright side of things. She focused on the fact that we still had our father with us. She found support through family and church. Since my mother needed to stay home with my father, money was tight, yet we still went on vacation every year to visit our cousins, which included a trip to the nearby seashore. We didn't have every toy and item we wanted, but when the topic came up, she explained that we just didn't have the money, and I accepted that. I have wonderful memories of my youth, and I never focused on the negative because my mother's positive approach really changed the entire way I viewed my circumstances. She didn't blame anyone for the past, and she took control of the future. As I became a mother with my own children, I realized how difficult that time must have been for my mother, and I still marvel at how she was able to stay positive and model such great messages to her children. To this day, I have wonderful memories of my childhood and feel inspired by the way my mother continued to live her best life and provide a happy place for her children during such a difficult time in her own life. Her actions have inspired me as a mom and reminded me that life is what you make it and the choice is yours to make. Now as you read the rest of the stories from moms and children around the world, I hope they will warm your heart and inspire you along the way!

INSPIRING STORIES FROM THE HEART

Miles of Memories

L.S., California, USA

Moms are memory makers. We stay up till 4 a.m. wrapping Santa's gifts only to be woken up a few hours later to the task of cleaning up a thousand yards of torn wrapping paper and ribbons, assembling doll houses and bicycles, putting batteries in everything and, oh yes, let's not forget the intricate holiday meal that awaits her skills in the kitchen. Or how about the family trip to the lake that the children remember as wonderful lazy days by the water and smores over the campfire each night, while mom spent a week packing the gear, planning the meals, doing the shopping, doing a master Tetris job on getting everything into the car, and while the family was enjoying a vacation, she was working to give it to them.

Moms are selfless doers. Some of my favorite memories involved time with my grandparents, aunts, uncles, and cousins. We had a blast with sleepovers and pool days. As a child, I didn't pay any attention to the work the adults were putting into these events. I just thoroughly enjoyed them. So when I became a parent, I knew making sure my kids made memories with their extended family was of the utmost importance. The problem was I lived 437 miles away.

Moms find a way. When my kids were 5, 3, and 1, I bought a silver Toyota Corolla. I was a newly single mother, going through a lot of emotional stress, but this car represented a great deal. It was the first major purchase I made on my own, and it was going to be our vessel for a life of adventure and memories. I was determined their upbringing was not going to be lacking just because their dad and I had parted ways. Taking a road trip home seemed to meet multiple needs. I could spend some time with my family for my own support, and my kids could spend time with their family and make those memories I considered so vital to their childhood. So, I picked up my babies and packed up my Corolla, and we set out on our 437-mile adventure. And what an adventure it turned out to be!

Moms are relentless. For the next 12 years, we made this trip 4-5 times a year. That road trip has become a defining part of our lives. Some of it amazing, like listening to my oldest son sing along with the soundtrack to *Mama Mia,* which he hates but has memorized because it's his sister's favorite. Some less amazing, like the countless times I've been pulled over on the side of the interstate with a car sick child. (By the way, the method for learning if your child gets car sick is to take a trip and see if they vomit all over themselves, their car seat, and your upholstery. This is especially entertaining if you yourself have a sensitive constitution and must attempt to clean everyone and everything up while taking breaks to dry heave so that you don't add to the messy problem.) The reward, though, proved priceless. My kids remember their summers as being spent in Grandma's pool or on the beach building sandcastles with their aunties. They grew up playing board games, dress-up, and Wii bowling with their cousins. My youngest son will forever tell the Thanksgiving story of making a tur-duck-en with my brother-in-law. And I personally cherish the memory of me and the kids dancing the night away at my cousin's wedding. Every mile on that road was worth it for the memories and for the life we built.

Moms are teachers. As we packed the car for one of our trips, the kids were dreading the drive. "Mom, why do we have to do this drive all the time?" It was a fair question and one I often asked myself as I was holding my eyelids open with toothpicks to finish the last grueling hour of the drive. I simply replied, "We do what we have to for family. It's how we show we love each other." That seemed to satisfy their little brains, but I had no idea how it would stick with them. My kids are now teenagers, practically adults, and I get to witness the fruits of my road trip labor every day. My oldest is a typical young man, in his own world, focused on himself, and not too concerned with anybody else at the moment. When he graduated during the coronavirus pandemic, he accepted the virtual ceremony with ease, but he absolutely insisted on celebrating with family. My daughter is that cool, older cousin all the younger cousins look up to. She carries on the banner of strong, intelligent women from a family of five aunties, a grandmother, and a great grandmother who are all magnificent matriarchs. And my youngest is the heir to our traditions, the consummate entertainer and family favorite. He is always there to help when it's needed. In a metaphoric passing of the torch, the three of them recently took a road trip to Grandma's house ON THEIR OWN! I was of course terrified, but they have labeled it the best road trip they've ever taken, and for three teenagers to actually have enjoyed each other's company, that much is a miracle in itself! Most impressive is how they can come together as a force of love without even knowing it. When a couple who had acted as pseudo parents to me after my divorce passed away, I was not only filled with grief but also a flood of painful memories from a difficult time in my life. I wanted to go and pay my respects at the memorial service, but I didn't have the strength to go on my own. I humbly asked the kids if they'd go with me. I had no idea what they'd say and assumed a funeral for people they can't remember would feel awkward and so not cool. Without hesitation, these teenagers were there for me, voluntary dressed in the clothes they hate to wear, and held my hand through the entire service. They get it—we do what we have to for family.

Moms are there for each other. Mothering is hard work. And sometimes, it is years before you see the results of that work. Take heart, mammas, those beautiful kids are taking in everything you are dishing out. The work, the wait, and the worry are all worth it.

From Homeless to Home

J.N., Germany

I remember the one summer night when we were sleeping in our car—it feels like it was so long ago. My dad died suddenly and my mom couldn't keep up with the bills because we lived in a big city and the rent was high. She decided that if we moved to a smaller town, we could have a better life and not struggle so much. I remember watching her sitting at the kitchen table and planning our move. She had a notebook and pen, and she made lists and timelines, all the while keeping a positive attitude. She would talk about the parks we would go to and the yard we could play in. She told us about the new school friends that we would meet, and she really helped to make us feel excited about our new life.

One day, she sat down with me and explained how she wrote down all the little steps we would need to take and that if we followed each step, even though some of them may be a bit difficult, we could get to the country dream that we were holding inside. She explained that when we first left, we would travel by car and may need to sleep in the car for a few days until we got settled in our new town.

I was a bit nervous but she seemed so positive that things would work out, so I just put my trust in her. She had been communicating with people in this town while looking for a job and a place to live. We arrived in the town, and she smiled and told us that we made it! She said there were just a few more things to attend to and we would be on our way to our dreams. We pulled into a gas station and she went into the bathroom and returned in her finest dress. She looked beautiful! We then drove to a small area with shops and a park nearby. She told us we could play at the park, and she would be right back because she had a job interview. She came back smiling, looked at her watch, and let us know that we could play for a bit more, but then she had something exciting to show us.

We got back in the car and headed down a long rode with lots of trees. When we stopped, there was a man and lady standing out front of the cutest small house I had ever seen. We went in and mom looked around and then handed the woman some money, and the woman handed mom a key. That night we spent the night laying on blankets in our newly rented home. We enrolled in school, and little by little, we furnished the house with second-hand furniture. The yard was beautiful, just like my mom described when she was sitting at the kitchen table making her plans. Step by step, the picture that my mom created in my imagination slowly came to reality. We had a wonderful life there. Over time, I made so many friends. My mom loved her job, and our house became a home.

As I became a mother myself in that same little town, I thought back over that time and wondered how my mother was ever strong enough to make that journey. I knew she must have been frightened to make such a big move with two young children. One day, as she was visiting my house, I asked her about that time and she told me she was terrified but knew that if she had a step-by-step plan, was open to adjusting it as she hit bumps along the way, and stayed positive for her kid's sake, things had to work out in the end. She said she just kept that image of our home and happy lives in her head and that by sharing it with us, it helped her see her dream before it even came true.

I marvel at my mom and her strength and all the lessens I learned from that experience. I learned to face my fears, start with little steps, stay positive, and keep moving toward my dreams, even if they seem very far away. All those lessons have helped me many times in my life, and I am blessed to have them to fall back on. Now I use them to reach my own dreams, because I learned from my mom that nothing is impossible!

Grandmother's Dream

C.G., Venezuela

This is a story about my grandmother. She taught me to never give up on my dreams, to be perseverant, and that with hard work, anything you want, can be possible.

About sixty years ago, when most of the women in our society didn't or weren't allowed to work, let alone dream of starting their own business, my grandmother, a mother of seven children, in the middle of a complicated marriage, decided it was time to do something for herself, for her dreams.

She wanted to own her own business, but she didn't have much money at the time, so she started to save money, little by little. She saved anything possible, until she had enough to rent a little corner space to start selling anything she could. She started by selling groceries, sodas, and even sandwiches that she prepared herself. For some people, it might have appeared as if it was something little, but for her, it was just the beginning of her dream.

At the time, she may have felt as if the world was not in her favor, that she didn't have many possibilities to succeed in a time when a woman that was a business owner wasn't very common, but she didn't let that make her lose hope.

My grandmother didn't know how to properly do the math to start her own business. It wasn't usual for a woman to go to school at the time, so she never did. She grew up in the countryside, only learning the basics of everything, like reading and writing, but she didn't experience much more than that.

She grew up in a family that had some money at the time, so she never felt like she would need to work to earn her own money to survive, but life circumstances made her realize she had to work to support herself, even if the odds weren't in her favor. She had the help of her kids to learn the things she didn't have the opportunity to learn when she was little, so her eldest daughter, my aunt, who was studying at the time, taught her mother about math. With love and patience, they joined forces to keep fighting for my grandmother's dreams.

I remember my grandmother being a kind-hearted person. She always had a nice word to say to everyone, and she wanted to help as many people as she could. Even then, when she was starting to grow her own business, and she didn't have much to offer herself, she couldn't help but try to offer help to the people who walked by her store.

Students and workers often walked by her store on their way back home after a long day at school or work. When someone didn't have enough money to buy a sandwich or get a glass of fresh juice, she just gave it to them, asking for nothing in return. When someone had money to buy only a couple of slices of cheese, she just put some extra slices in their bag, or if a person entered to buy just a loaf of bread, sometimes she gave them two. She always liked to help other people. She felt that if she could make anyone's day a bit easier, then her entire mission on this earth was accomplished.

She liked to listen to her customers, to talk to them after the long hours of the day or in the first hours in the morning before they went to school or work. She gave them advice and was someone who listened to them and to their problems and misfortunes. She was someone with warm motherly energy that made everyone around her feel at home.

Little by little, the store started to grow. Her customers spread the word to others, and the place got fuller and fuller each day, so she had to rent the area next door. After a while, she was able to purchase the building. She was so happy she finally owned something that she purchased with her own earned money. With time, they had more things to sell, and each day, she could see her dream starting to come true in front of her eyes.

The big shelves placed on the walls of the establishment had not only food as when she started, but now they also offered stationery supplies, clothing items, shoes, makeup, and anything you could think of. There was a little bit of everything around the store, which reflected the real treasures found inside.

All the family started to help in the business as they got busier. My mother, aunts, and uncles helped her clean the store, organize the shelves, and restock everything. She taught them to work, to help, and to be kind with anyone who walked through the door.

My grandmother worked very hard every single day. She got up early in the morning to prepare everything in the store, and she went to bed late at night, cleaning and doing the bookkeeping. She liked to work in the store herself. She wasn't afraid of doing any hard work that was needed. She enjoyed talking to her customers and preparing meals behind the counter, and she loved to give them free items and to see the expression on their faces as well.

The store kept growing, and it got to the point that she owned the entire corner of that street. She had regular providers coming in each week, lots of customers, and a beautiful space she had created herself, starting from nothing. She was so proud she could provide for her family and own her business. She created a magnificent store out of nowhere, with perseverance and hard work.

Of all the stories she told me about the store, her favorite moments came from Christmas time. My grandmother adored Christmas, and she wanted to share her joy with everybody else, so during the month of December, she made a list and included all the children who lived in the area, and she decided to get them all presents for Christmas Day. She told me they stayed up all night for several days wrapping up presents and organizing everything for the children, but that it was all worth it when she saw their faces light up when they received their unexpected gift.

She became a very important person in their community, who won hearts with kindness and a smile. She ran her business responsibly. She made sure everything ran perfectly, and as the years went by, she was able to send her children to university with the money that she earned in that store. She was also able to buy a house with her profits, a loving home for her and her family to live in.

My grandmother always taught me to work hard for my dreams. She always said that it didn't matter if I wanted to become a business owner, a doctor, a singer, or a writer (which I ended up being), as long as I worked every day to accomplish my goals and tried to be the best I could be. She told me that anything is possible if you truly believe in it, that no dream is too big and no goal is too far when you really want it and put in effort to get it. But most importantly, I think she taught me to see the best in everything, to not let myself get knocked down by obstacles, and to face every difficulty that life may throw at me with a smile on my face and a kind heart.

My grandmother's story taught me that no matter what the circumstances were, there's always time and space to help others, to make anybody's day a bit easier, and to give something to someone who may need it without expecting anything in return. She taught me we all can make the world a better place if we show just a little bit of kindness every day.

One of the things I remember the most about my grandmother was her beautiful smile. I don't recall ever seeing her angry or annoyed by any trouble, and she always seemed to face life with joy and laughter. She had the ability to lighten up a room and make everyone forget about their problems in an instant. No matter how difficult the situation was or how crazy the dream appeared, she was always there to show support, provide a word of encouragement, and help others chase their dreams as she once did.

What I learned most from my grandmother was to never give up, to go after what I want in life, and to not be afraid of the obstacles standing between me and my dreams. She also taught me that anything is possible, to never stop smiling, and to always believe in myself and in my dreams!

A Birthday to Remember

A.R., Florida, USA

My birthdays had never been good. I believed that the 14th of November was destined to be bad. Something would happen every year, and no matter how hard I tried to be happy, it always ended in disaster. So, on the days leading up to my 16th birthday, I knew something was going to happen. I tried to think of every possible scenario that could ruin it, and then I tried to come up with every and any possible solution. I was determined to finally have a good day.

On November 11th, my friends kept on reminding me that I was going to turn 16 and that was when I could start applying for jobs and be a little more grown up.

The morning of November 14th, I was awakened by the music of "Happy Birthday." It was something that my dad always played when it was someone's birthday. It brought a smile to my face because it gave me a strand of hope. Maybe this year would be a birthday that wouldn't turn out so bad. I went to school, and many people wished me a happy birthday. I was a little disappointed that no one gave me any gifts, not even my friends I saw at school. That feeling clung to me for the rest of the school day, and it started making me feel worse about myself. I kind of felt guilty because the "Happy Birthdays" didn't feel enough. If anything, I wanted something that made me feel loved and appreciated like everyone was telling me.

When I got home that day, I didn't think my brother was having a good day, and I felt he was projecting it onto me. He decided to play his drums nonstop for at least 10 minutes. I went to his room to ask him to stop, and as siblings often do, he looked me dead in my eyes and responded with a stern no. I went into my room and laid down. The drumming of my brother's drums kept interrupting my thoughts and cutting into them. As I stared up at the ceiling, I thought about everything. It wasn't until I felt tears staining my cheeks and making their journey around my face that I got up.

I was crying. But why? Stupid emotions, I told myself. I hated spilling tears because this happened every year like a repetitive pattern.

The truth was it didn't feel like my birthday. I didn't feel loved or appreciated. I didn't feel that the people in my life thought I was a blessing. It made me feel even worse because I tried very hard to give my friends heartfelt gifts on their birthdays, and they did not reciprocate. In all my years of turning another year, I could not name a successful birthday, and it made me want to crawl into a hole for the rest of the day. I wanted November 14th to be over, and I wanted to skip that day every year after that.

My mother came home that day with bags from the store. The bags were from Family Dollar, and she called me into her room to show me what she got for me. At that time, she didn't have a car or a driver's license, so she had to walk to and from the store, which took 30 minutes. She revealed a bag of cookies and a card. I felt like I was going to cry, and just the fact that it was something so simple made me feel really stupid.

But the cookies and the card made my day. My mother looked disappointed and confessed that this was all she could get since she didn't have a job or car. But I didn't care. This was the best birthday present ever. The card read how much she loved me and wished I had a full life of blessings, and I couldn't help but cry again. I felt very loved and treasured. The fact that she did something when no one else did made me cherish that moment.

This simple act still resonates with me today. Although she's in a better place now, I still have that letter, and no gift can compare to that card and the box of cookies. If she was still here today, I know it would surprise her that this special memory still touches my heart, and we would probably laugh about it and go out and buy those cookies again.

She inspires me, and it shows me that sometimes we don't need extravagant things, just thoughtful things.

Sweet Intentions

K.L., Italy

I was at my wit's end! After many chaotic school mornings in our household, I decided enough was enough. I had to take a minute to plan and get things better organized. I was tired of lost items, running late, and the stress that ensued. I called my three school age children into the room for a meeting, while my 4-year-old was having a quiet moment drawing. I let them know that from that moment on, the mornings would run much more smoothly. I set up a small area rug and gave each child a spot to put their school items. I told them that all items for the following day were to be set by the door before bedtime each evening. There was pushback at first, but after we started discussing the reasons for this and how it would make the morning start out much more smoothly, they started to come around. They even suggested some of their own ideas about how we could organize things. My oldest son brought out a file holder for his homework from his room and put it on the shelf near the door. What began as a conversation, which I must admit had started with a bit of a stressed-out attitude, ended in total agreement! I was pleased.

The next week went well, the mornings were smooth, and everyone was on time. I was even feeling a bit proud of myself for finally taking a stand and not putting up with the daily disorganization we were accustomed to. The following Monday, when the older kids were in school, I sent my 4-year-old to her room to pick up her toys before lunch. I went to the kitchen to find something to make for lunch and when I returned, I was surprised that my daughter had picked up many of her toys, but I also noticed a new pile of about five items near the door. When I asked her about them, she explained that those were the things that she needed during the day. She explained that she didn't want to forget them or be late if she couldn't find them when she needed them.

In the pile, she included a pair of her undies, her hairbrush, a pair of old shoes from her closet, and her favorite toy bear. There was one other item that puzzled me—it was a crumpled-up piece of blue construction paper.

When I asked her what that was for, she said, "Sometimes we do things during the day that make me so happy that I want to make you a card to say thank you, and I don't want to have to look all over to find something to make it with."

I melted as I realized that not only did my youngest child learn from watching my interaction with my older children, but she displayed the sweetest intentions while doing so.

My Mother's Touch

L.G., Jamaica

At the tender age of six, my mom was sent to live with her father's sister. She stayed with her aunt until she was 17. Her aunt's house was more home to her than that of her parents. When my parents met, they had a whirlwind romance, and at the age of 20, my mom found herself alone and pregnant with her second child. By the time she found out she was having me, my father had travelled for work, not knowing anything of my impending entrance into the world. With no job, no husband, and no prospects, she did what everyone does when the world knocks you down. She went home. She seemed to be searching for love, so shortly after that, she met and moved in with a handsome young man. I joined them in the home soon after, and he was the person I would call Daddy. By the time my second birthday rolled around, my mom was again pregnant with her third child. Life in rural Jamaica was sometimes hard. My stepdad went out to earn for his growing family, and my mom tended to the home. Our house may not have been the richest, but there was laughter and there was love. My first memory was of my mom writing on a blackboard and teaching me and my younger sister to spell our names. I still remember asking her why my name was different from my sisters, which was when she told me that I had a different father.

Even though life was sometimes hard, Mummy allowed us to be kids and to not think about these hardships of life. I can recall her watching us from the doorway and smiling at our laughter and joy as we ran around in the rain. Her love for us was something fierce. She would stand at the gate each evening until we returned home from school. When I think of those days, I feel warm and I know that's what a mother's love is. I have always wanted to make her proud of me, so I studied and I stayed focused on my schoolwork because she would often say she wanted us to make something of ourselves. She once told me how a group of young women laughed at her as she walked by holding the hands of my young sister and me all the while being heavily pregnant with her third child. To this day, if you ask her about that experience, a dark cloud rolls across her face. She would always say you are not ready to date until you have a job and the keys to your own door. For this reason, I waited until I was 32 to have my first and only child.

The union between my mother and stepdad became strained in the 12th year of my life. She found the inner strength to move out on her own with her kids in tow. She managed to secure a job as a chef at a local hotel. She has always been our biggest cheerleader; this woman believes in me and my abilities more than I believe in myself. On the first day of my very first big exam to exit high school, I woke up early trying to cram more things into my already saturated brain. She said, "Rest your mind, little girl. You are going to do great." She lovingly touched my shoulder as she left for work, and I calmed down and went on to do just what she said—great. Another instance, I was feeling so sad and alone in university. This was my first time leaving home and living away from her. I called her crying saying, "I don't even know why you sent me here. I can't do this." That was one of the first times I experienced her tough love. She let me know I was bigger than anything I would face out there, and I could do anything I put my mind to. She told me to stop acting like I wasn't because she knew I was smart from the first time I moved across her belly. She used to read to me, and she often recalls and is happy to tell anyone how even before I could speak, I was trying to read. That weekend, she sent one of my little sisters to visit me so I wouldn't be homesick.

My mom has always been an inspiration to me. Her struggles, her prayers, and her love have made me into the woman I am today. She was always open and honest about her struggles as she didn't want her daughters to have to go through the same things she went through. She sacrificed so much and went to bed without meals so we could go to school the next day. She always saw education as a way out of poverty, so she made sure we could all read and write. My mom has five children: one a carpenter, two entrepreneurs, a nurse, and my little brother, the youngest, is a master diver. We all wanted to give back so she could experience the best life has to offer and enjoy all the things she couldn't when she was younger. I know we make her proud because I still catch her smiling wistfully at one or all of us. No one will ever laugh at my mom's expense ever again.

Negative to Positive

M.K., Washington D.C., USA

I must admit, I used to be a very negative person, and I didn't see it at first. I guess it was because I had been that way for quite some time and that was just my normal way of thinking. That started to change after reading the first chapter of *The Power of Moms with Dreams*. I started to become much more aware of how I viewed things in my daily life. It really hit me when I observed my four-year-old daughter as she played with her doll. It appeared that she was imitating me as she pretended to come home from work, and I must admit, it was not pretty. She pretended she just walked in the door from her job. She then complained to her doll about her exhausting day at work and how tired she was. She said she didn't feel like making dinner because "no one would probably eat it anyway." I couldn't believe what I heard. I thought back over the many times I said that exact thing as I came home from work and was horrified that at such a young age, she had picked up on it all! I decided right then and there that it was time for me to be more positive. As our family sat at the dinner table that night, I suggested that we each share with the rest of the family one happy thing that happened that day. The kids had a little trouble coming up with something at first, but they seemed to like the conversation, so we continued to do this each day. Every day it seemed to get easier and easier for everyone to come up with their good news, and before long, the older children came to the dinner table eager to share their good news without any prompting at all.

While the dinner sharing was a quick success, it took a little more time for me to remain positive throughout the entire day, but I continued to work at it. I started by looking for something positive every time I caught myself being negative, which was often at first. It was a bit forced in the beginning, but I noticed how it kept getting easier and easier. I also noticed how focusing on positivity made me feel better.

One day when my four-year-old and I were going to the grocery store, I remembered about the Goodness Game that I read about in the book. I taught her how to play, and we had fun on the way as we pointed out people who were doing something nice for themselves or others. She really enjoyed it. About three weeks later, I was making dinner and thinking about how I was really starting to notice more positivity in my life, and my daughter was again playing with her doll. I could not believe the change in her. She was talking away and speaking so lovingly to her doll. At one point, she sat her doll in a small chair and said, "Come on, honey. We are going to the grocery store; it will be fun. We will play the Goodness Game on the way and look for all the good things people do." At that moment, I realized that I was starting to impact my child's happiness and her positive outlook on life, just by making such a small change in my own life. Looking for the positive in my life was not only helping me, but it was making our whole family happier!

Perseverance and Strength

J.M., China

I was born in a small mountain village, which is very far from the county seat. The ancestors seldom left the village. They lived by farming, so the conditions were tough. When I was eight years old, I had to carry about twenty kilograms of luggage to go to school in another village. It took about three to four hours to get there. We had to travel on seven mountain roads after crossing several mountains. Yet this was not the most difficult thing. The most difficult thing was that I lived at the school continuously for 10 days, followed by four days of holiday. This continued for six years. At that time, the communication there was underdeveloped and there was no telephone. At the beginning, I cried every day and missed my parents very much. It was difficult for me because I was so young. Every time I went home, I cried and didn't want to go back to school. At that time, my mother told me it was best for me to keep going and she hoped that someday I would understand. No matter how much I cried, the routine of days at school and days at home continued.

Although I did not adapt at the beginning, I did become more comfortable as time passed. I persisted for six years until I graduated from junior high school. Now looking back, I see that I gained tremendously from my persistence during those six years. I now realize that through that exposure and years of education, I have been given the strength to work hard and the opportunity to broaden my life experience. I realize that it provided me with the skills to go out and explore a wider world. In life, my ability to take care of myself is stronger. I noticed that many of my classmates depended on their parents for so much, even after they were college students. I began to feel strong and independent. I became proud of myself.

My mother's dream of providing me with the strength and skills to achieve my own goals took hold. Step by step, I was able to move out of my village, out of my county, and out of my city. I am now able to experience more opportunity and expand my world. Now that I have children of my own, I will make certain that they know the lessons that I learned through my mother's love, that perseverance is strength and life is what you make it!

Never Too Late

K.P., Texas, USA

Throughout my whole life, I always dreamed of being an attorney. I used to watch court shows when I was young and imagine I was in the court room right along with them. Well, things didn't go quite the way I had planned, and during my third year of college, I became pregnant with my son. I experienced every emotion including sadness, embarrassment, shame, disappointment, anger, and especially fear. At the time, I thought the best thing that I could do was to move back home and get a job in my hometown to support myself and my baby. I submitted applications everywhere I could and was relieved to finally get a job offer. I started a job in a local bank and put my dream of being an attorney aside. Once I dealt with my initial emotions, I started to feel better about my decisions and proud that I was able to support my child. I decided that regardless of the circumstances, I was going to continue living the best life I knew how. It was difficult being a single parent and taking care of my baby while working to pay all my expenses. I was so busy at first that I didn't realize how much I missed my old life and dreams, but I wouldn't give up my son for the world.

As years went by and my son became a teenager, I was talking with my boss one day. I shared how I had always wanted to be an attorney. She asked me why I wasn't doing it. I explained to her that my son was my priority and when he is grown, I would be too old, along with a million other excuses and fears that were stopping me. She listened and then told me to not give up yet and told me that it was never too late to follow my dreams. As days went by, I couldn't get the thought of going back to school out of my mind. Why couldn't I live my dream and be there for my son?

Long story short, I went to the nearby college and finally started my journey toward the career of my dreams, and you know what? One day when my son was in high school and was struggling with a school project he was working on, I made the comment that I was proud of how dedicated he was. He said, "Thanks, but I got it from you." When I asked what he meant, he explained that he watched me work hard to take care of the house and him and still make time to do fun things together, all while going back to school to follow my dreams. He said he saw how happy and dedicated I was and told me that if I can do all that, he can surely work hard on one assignment because he has dreams too, and I was proof that he can reach them. He told me that I taught him that just because something seemed hard to do or scared him a bit, it didn't have to keep him from his happiness. Then he told me he was proud to have me as his mom. I'm in tears writing this story because I am so happy that I didn't let fear and obstacles stop me, because not only did it change my life for the better, but it also changed my son's.

Loving and Strong

N.Z., Australia

My mother hated her wedding dress. It had ugly layered ruffles and a bloated skirt. I like to tell her she looked more like the wedding cake than the actual cake did. My grandmother was the one who picked out the dress. I asked my mum, "If you could go back in time, would you have stood up to your mother and worn a different dress?"

"No," she had told me. "I would have stood up to my mother and married a different man."

Eight years after her marriage, she had two children: an eight-year-old girl and a four-year-old boy. Eight years later, she couldn't do it anymore.

My mother worked two jobs, one full-time retail job and another part-time job. Between work and home life, she barely had time to rest her feet. My mother never talked of big goals or aspirations involving her career or life; she only longed for one thing. She always wanted children, specifically three. Her two children had a four-year age gap, as she wanted some time in between; however, she wanted her youngest child to be closer in age to her middle child. Unfortunately her husband, my father, did not wish to have more children.

My mother became pregnant, and one day my mother and father began arguing. My father threatened to hit her. Although they had argued, he had never hit her or done anything physical before. Suddenly, he struck her on the cheek. For a few moments, she remained still like she was in shock.

This was the last straw. She grabbed us and put us into the car. He told her not to leave. I'm pretty sure she was tempted to run him over at that moment, but she didn't. Instead, she drove to my grandmother's house. When she arrived to see my grandmother, my grandmother was very upset at the sight. My mom's right eye had swelled significantly and was a purple hue. When she was taken to the doctor, she was informed that her cheek had a slight fracture.

It was a stressful period in our lives. My mom continued her two jobs, rented a house for us, informed friends and family about the separation, and continued to provide us with an abundance of love.

It didn't take long for her to settle into her new role as a single mother. After all, it didn't feel different from what she had been doing before. But she was dealing with constant stress and had even lost weight despite being pregnant. She was then told that her baby had a common defect called a cleft lip and palate. She continued to be strong and knew that her baby would be greatly loved and well cared for.

Throughout her pregnancy, she continued to work. It wasn't in her nature to stop, no matter how far along she was. Then the hospital told her she had to stop working, as it was too risky. My grandmother often visited us to help out when she could. She kept reminding us about how strong a woman our mother was. Even at our younger ages, we were so proud of our mother and the things she did for her family.

Eighteen years later, she never remarried, but instead happily devoted her time and energy to her work and her children, and we all learned so much about life from her. It must have been difficult for her to leave when she was pregnant with two young children, but she taught us to have dignity for ourselves even though it was a struggle financially, physically, and emotionally. She taught us that life is what you make it, things can get better, and no one deserves to be hit. I am the only child who still lives with her at this time. My brother moved out a few years ago but still visits Mum and me often, and my sister lives with her boyfriend and 2-year-old daughter. We learned so much from watching everything that our mom did to take care of us and keep us safe. She is a role model to all of us. My sister is now raising her own young child, and when people describe my sister, the words they use most are friendly, funny and most of all strong. I think she likes being called that best, because it reminds her of our mum, and now she looks forward to being the same strong-willed role model for her daughter that our mother was to us.

I'vE Got This

V.B., Canada

I am V.B., a mommy of two little darlings (five years old and 10 months old), a finance professional, and an entrepreneur, working to make my dreams into reality. My five-year-old son observed me very closely during my not-so-smooth pregnancy, commuting for two hours daily, working long hours in my job, participating in trade shows for my business, and spending every hour I possibly could (when I was home) smiling and playing with him. He has seen me planning and making lists for things I have to and want to do. He has seen me and my husband accepting the situation, making the most of it, and me murmuring to myself, "I got this."

And then, with a new addition in our family and due to a pandemic, we have been 24/7 learning and growing together. Instead of complaining about the situation, I am noticing my little inquisitive trooper accepting the situation, being an excellent big brother, enjoying virtual schooling, wanting to learn new things, writing daily plans, and crossing them off one by one. You will often hear my little guy saying things like *strategy*, *action plan*, and *let's do this one by one*.

And when times get tough and I break down, he is the one who hugs me and says exactly what I say to him, "It's ok, Mummy. I am here, we can do it, I will help you, just hug me tight." And before learning to ride a bicycle or even doing a cartwheel, I hear him say, "I got this."

My son has been the inspiration behind my business, Panchhi Inc., to create non-toxic and 100% chemical-free essentials to nurture babies in the softness of organic cotton muslin and wellness of therapeutic herbal dyes. I don't know what heights I will take my business to, but one thing I am sure of: seeing my zest for life and desire to keep working on my dreams will inspire my kids to take risks in the future and to not give up easily.

BE YOURSELF

F.F., Pakistan

Greetings! I'd like to tell you an inspirational story about my mom. I'd like to tell you about how my mom inspired me and my siblings throughout life, but first let me give you a brief overview about the background of the traditions and customs about education where she lived. I will then relate that context to my mom and her story of how she managed to get her education from scratch and how me and my siblings were inspired by her. The city that we are from used to be a very backward area of Pakistan, and the people at the time when my mother was young were mostly uneducated and the literacy rate was very low. Most people didn't pay attention to formal studies at that time. My mother told us how her cousins were able to get admission to a school for their studies, but their parents took them out of the school. That was a time when there was much illiteracy and crime. It was the 1990s when she started her education, and she somehow managed to get through that era, but it was very tough for her. My grandparents didn't let her attend school very easily. She remembered sitting in a corner of her room and crying because she wanted to pursue her education. I am very inspired by my mother because of her struggles in life. When she reached her higher secondary education, she got married and things became more difficult for her. She told us she that she always had an interest in her studies, reading novels and books, and gaining knowledge. She knew that inspiration was the key for a successful lifestyle. She told us that when we love, we always strive to become better than we are, and when we strive to become better than we are, everything around us becomes better too. After my mom was married, her marriage made it more difficult to continue with her studies, but she believed that change was the result of all true learning. So, she kept trying hard to complete her higher education. I know she was doing it for us, for her children, and we admire her a lot for that. When things were hard for our family, she wanted to help us with everything she could. She worked as a teacher to get us the money for our education, even when there was pressure from the family not to work. She was eager to help us thrive, and we will always be grateful.

When I was one year old, she fed me and bathed me. I thanked her by crying all night long. When I was two years old, she taught me to walk. I thanked her by running away when she called. When I was three years old, she made all my meals with love. I thanked her by tossing my plate on the floor. When I was four years old, she gave me some crayons. I thanked her by coloring the dining room table. When I was five years old, she dressed me for the holidays. I thanked her by plopping into the nearest pile of mud. When I was six years old, she walked me to school. I thanked her by screaming, "I'M NOT GOING!" When I was seven years old, she bought me a baseball. I thanked her by throwing it through the next-door-neighbor's window. When I was eight years old, she handed me an ice cream. I thanked her by dripping it all over my lap. When I was nine years old, she paid for piano lessons. I thanked her by never even bothering to practice. When I was 10 years old, she drove me all day, from soccer to gymnastics to one birthday party after another. I thanked her by jumping out of the car and never looking back. When I was 11 years old, she took me and my friends to the movies. I thanked her by asking to sit in a different row. When I was 12 years old, she warned me not to watch certain TV shows. I thanked her by waiting until she left the house. Those teenage years! When I was 13, she suggested a haircut that was becoming. I thanked her by telling her she had no taste. When I was 14, she paid for a month away at summer camp. I thanked her by forgetting to write a single letter. When I was 15, she came home from work, looking for a hug. I thanked her by having my bedroom door locked. When I was 16, she taught me how to drive her car. I thanked her by taking it every chance I could. When I was 17, she was expecting an important call. I thanked her by being on the phone all night. After all these things, I realize that what she had done for us could never be paid in our lifetime, and we took too much time to realize that. Now that I am experienced and more engaged with things, I surely know that my role model is my mom. She is a true inspirational character for me. She completed her education while overcoming so many difficulties, and now she is a speech therapist and a makeup artist as well, while running a salon business on the side. When I look at her, I see success. I followed her ways and now I am also successful, and I am in my dream university because of her. Let us take a moment of time just to pay tribute and show appreciation to the person called Mom, though some may not say it openly to their mother. There's no substitute for her. Cherish every single moment. I remember as a young child, times were financially hard in our family. I remember when I wanted a phone for my studies, so I collected money from working and teaching students, but it still didn't match up with the price, so my mom sold her gold earrings to be certain that I had enough to buy my phone. Mom would sometimes have to borrow my allowance money to make ends meet at the end of the week. Still once a month, she would buy some steaks and would grill them up for Dad and me (she knew I loved steak), and she would end up giving me half of hers because I would want more. I was too young to completely understand what she was doing. But now as I am more mature, I understand the sacrifices she made for us. For my brother, my sister, and me, *Guitar Hero* was a competition of who could score the most points on the hardest level. Mom, on the other hand, would play the ten-minute "Freebird" on the easiest level while we kids prepared for our next showdown. When Mom restarted the song after missing a note, we all shouted our disapproval. "Rock stars do what they want," she said, and we laughed because we agreed: Mom was a rock star. At one point, it was mid-January and a huge snowstorm hit the area. The snow was so thick, the highways came to a complete stop. We lived a half of a block from the highway. The darkness of night was approaching and all seven of us kids were keeping warm inside. There were several cars stuck with people and their families and pets inside. Mom stood up and said to my brother, "I will open my house to the stranded people on the highway." She said, "Please go to them and invite them to our house." We had thirteen families come. Our living room was covered in sleeping bags, blankets, and pillows. In the morning, we had three pots of coffee, one huge pot of hot chocolate, bacon, eggs and warm French bread. Everyone showed such gratitude. Mom's act of kindness and humanity was so profound to me. She showed us all the selflessness of helping others—such a great personality I had never seen in my life. My mom had a great sense of humor and a knack for making everything fun. One thing that resonated with me, even as a small child, was how much she seemed to enjoy her own company and found ways to entertain herself. As a kid, I remember her giggling while paying bills. What was so funny about bill paying? She would put humorous notes in the reference section of the check: For the electric bill, she might put "You light up my life," and for the mortgage she'd write "Four shingles closer to owning it all." On the first day of first grade, I stood by the front door with butterflies in my stomach. I voiced my biggest concern to my mother: "How will I make friends?" Crouching in front of me, she handed me advice I carry with me to this day: "Be yourself. Be friends with everyone. Treat everyone equally and fairly." For all of my 20 years, I have lived by these words. Soon I will graduate and become a part of the real world. And on that first day, nervously facing new responsibilities, I know I will whisper the words to myself: "Be what my mom was."

Let's Empower Our Kids

A.C., South Africa

When I fell pregnant with my eldest, I knew that I wanted to be with my children. Not for me, but them! Because kids learn best from what they see, it is an amazing opportunity for us as moms to be their role models when they are highly susceptible and curious to learn. I knew that I had to be the one to take care of their needs and teach them. Who knows our kids better than us? Who can be a better role model? It was extremely important to me that they always feel safe, and I knew that safety would build their confidence. I am the bridge to giving them that gift. But in the back of my mind, I knew that I also wanted to build a business again…

When my eldest son was born, I became very interested in natural vitamin C for our family's health. I knew that it was important to keep our immune systems strong naturally.

The journey to family health brought about my premium quality natural vitamin C business. Although I was struggling with business-family balance initially, I implemented different strategies to make time for the business and not to neglect my kids. Kids are always the first priority.

When I was a young girl, I had to go to a playgroup during the day. I remember vividly that all I wanted was to be close to my mom. Now I have the chance to give that gift to my kids and be there for them.

Whilst building a business would mean some compromises, I was OK with the fact that healthy compromises teach kids that life is not just always about a perfect comfort zone and always receiving, but that give-and-take is important for a healthy balance in life. Even though I was home with them, they would have to give up some time with me so that I could focus on my business, plus healthy boundaries would have to be set.

This meant that I had to learn how to structure my business, automate, plan my time effectively, and become even more disciplined to gain control over the business. One of the best decisions I made was to hire a nanny to free up a few hours for me to work and keep the kids occupied. The business soon became a semi-passive income business with little input. I was able to focus on my kids, join playgroups, homeschool them, and have a business on the side.

And it has paid off, big time! At the time of this writing, my kids are seven, five, and three. They are homeschooled, and they are confident! They spend only a fraction of the day on schoolwork, and when we face challenges, they tend to breeze through them. They are happy, and they feel secure!

Everywhere I go with them, moms ask me about being home with the kids and how it is possible to run my business effectively.

Everyone seems to have the same yearning: more time for kids and a dream of building their own business.

My heart started to resonate with these moms, so I started yet another business, and BizmomCoaching was born. The mission is to teach moms to have more time for their kids by structuring their businesses effectively, to show them what hard work within a balanced lifestyle looks like, but in the end, the impact is on their kids.

Their kids can see what happens when mom works hard but effectively. Their kids can experience the security of their moms being available to them. The kids can be confident and learn at their own pace – and they are also taught that boundaries and compromises are important to achieve success and balance in life.

As I immersed myself into the online business world of mom entrepreneurs, I came to realize that there were many common challenges that I have experienced while building my vitamin C business as a new mom.

I knew I could help other moms too, but little did I know that I too would have to go through the journey of overwhelm, procrastination, overworking, burn-out, lack of clarity and control, and some level of imposter syndrome in the new business model that I was unfamiliar with, before finding my footing properly.

I was trying so hard to learn everything about the coaching world and passive income streams by myself. This did not work! My time with my kids suffered, and I eventually had to admit defeat and enroll in business coaching courses to help me overcome many of those hurdles.

But then, life also happens. Sometimes things won't go as planned. And sometimes, life has a way of teaching us some of the lessons that we struggle to implement by ourselves.

I wanted to spend quality time with the kids every day.

I wanted to make time for self-care.

I wanted to get back into healthy eating. I wanted to exercise. But the business life was taking over, and none of this was happening like it used to, until it all changed...

The above yearnings were enforced upon me by a sudden and unexpected life event. It was something that shook me to the core, but in the end, it left me empowered and impacted my kids positively.

I was challenged with a sudden situation where I felt I had lost control over my body after I abruptly weaned my youngest. I still don't understand all the symptoms, but I was fine one moment, and then it felt like a rug was pulled from under my feet. Unfortunately, I did not understand what was happening at first (luckily, it was mainly hormonal adjustments - like, WHY isn't this common knowledge??), which sent me into a frenzy that spiraled into severe anxiety and panic attacks, tests, and numerous doctor appointments... I honestly thought there was something majorly wrong with me.

I could not invest time into my business while feeling so helpless, out of control, and mentally exhausted. Apart from fulfilling the main business priorities, my business stopped.

This was not an ideal situation to be in, but it was OK.

I have always believed that health is our number one priority in life. And apart from that, it is our kids. Health and kids should never suffer because of our work. If the business must wait so that we can take care of our health and our kids, I am OK with that! All the better if we show this principle to our kids through our actions.

It was especially hard to protect my kids from what I was experiencing. They were forced to go through the journey with me and see me at my lowest. The magical thing about this was that, once again, they handled the situation with such self-assurance, and they got to see that health really is important. They remained their happy, playful selves because we have built such a strong safety foundation. I once again realized that it was OK if kids see us go through hard times in life; we can come out the other end stronger.

I also learnt that it is better to be honest with our kids about what is going on at a level of their understanding. This gave them peace of mind and permission to just be themselves and trust the process.

Luckily with a financial security buffer and an amazing support structure, I managed to regain control and get back on my feet.

While it was an extremely hard time, the sun shone again.

The takeaway? It is important to have a buffer for hard times. Our kids must be empowered to move through difficult situations effortlessly. It was OK to take a break. It was OK to slow down. It was OK to take care of myself…and it was amazing to show my kids that it was.

I explained it to them like this: It is never fun to face hard challenges in life, but if we can learn valuable lessons from it and move forward with invaluable pearls of wisdom and grace, and apply lessons learned to create our best life yet, perhaps, it was all worth it.

I now had the opportunity to spend quality time with the kids every day again. I now had the opportunity to create time for self-care. I now had the opportunity to get back into healthy eating and to exercise.

I had the opportunity to change it all and live my best life while showing my kids how I do it.

I had the opportunity to show them that they can live their best lives, irrespective of what they are faced with.

After all, having our world shaken reminded me so much more that our kids are only small once – and I really didn't want to miss a thing!

And when all is said and done, I can show my kids that no situation is helpless after all. There is always positivity in every situation, and we are always empowered to choose our own paths. Challenges are an important part of the journey, but most importantly:

The best is yet to come. Always!

I Really Can

A.B., Pennsylvania, USA

One day, I was really frustrated with my life. I wasn't happy with where I was in life compared to where I wanted to be. I kept thinking about all the things that I didn't have, and I was focusing on this lack every day. I didn't want to have to always rent the home we lived in. I didn't want a job that I didn't feel happy or supported in. I didn't want to drive so far to work each day. I didn't want a job where I had to work on holidays and weekends. I didn't want to drive a car that broke down often. I would think about this on a weekly basis, and it was just making me exhausted. I felt stuck and didn't think that I could do anything about it. Growing up, I also heard people say that life is hard and you get what you work for. I didn't know how I could possibly work harder than I already was without collapsing. The only solutions seemed so out of reach to me, like winning the lottery, getting an inheritance, or marrying someone rich, but I was already married. So, day after day, those hopeless thoughts would swirl around in my head, making me feel powerless. On the rare occasion when I thought about doing something about it, I quickly became overwhelmed and defeated as what I now understand to be limiting thoughts came charging into my mind. I would think, I can't get a new job while I'm busy with my current job. We can't afford to buy a house of our own. I can't afford a better car. I won't ever get hired for a job that has weekends and holidays off. This went on for years, and then one day I was on my way to work, and my car quit in the middle of the highway. Another car hit it and totaled the car. Luckily, I was only slightly injured. I was in the hospital for a few days and a friend came to visit. I was telling her all about my tragic life, and she agreed that I did need things to get better. As she was talking to me, I again went through all the reasons why I couldn't have a better job, life, car, etc. She told me she just read a book that might help me and asked me not to get mad because she wanted to help me. I agreed because at this point, I had nothing left to try. As we talked and I continued to explain to her about my current life, I again brought up what I didn't want and couldn't have, and she stopped me each time and turned the sentence around with a question. She asked, "What DO you want?" I would then answer her question, but then add on the part about why I can't, won't, or don't have it. After some time of continually asking me why I can't or why I don't and why I won't, she helped me see that my reasons were not always logical, and some were even based on fear or past beliefs I had heard as a child. After that conversation, I began to pay attention to my use of the words "can't" or "don't" and started asking myself, *what do I want and what can I do?* This may seem simple, but it was the start of a better life for me. Once I knew what I wanted and realized that getting started by taking even the smallest first step would point me in the right direction, I felt so much better because I believed I had some control in my life.

Well, I took the first step and started with getting a better car. I researched about different types of cars, and since my car had been destroyed in the accident, I was going to receive insurance money to get another one. It was not quite the way I wanted that to happen, but I tried to look at this as an opportunity. Using the information I gained from my car research and the money from the insurance, I was able to purchase a car that was better suited to a daily drive. I then moved on to my job. I started to think that I could get a new job. I would just have to take the actions to get it, and I wouldn't have to do it all at once. I found it fun to do the research to find the job that met the list of requirements I had created for my dream job. I was surprised and motivated as I began searching the possibilities of jobs I could do that met my requirements.

I then found that the actual thought of finding a new job was worse than the act of finding a new job, and because I was inspired and motivated, I was having fun in the process.

As life was getting back to normal and I became excited about my future plans, I began sharing my story with my 13-year-old daughter. I started with the story of my friend telling me about negative and limiting statements that we all have and have used at some time in our lives. My daughter said that she was glad she rarely used them, and that was the end of our conversation that night. The next day, she came running in after softball practice and said that she couldn't believe how many times during the day she used negative words such as *can't* and *don't*. We decided we would both try to keep track of when we say them and ask ourselves the question my friend had asked me. We got to the point that we would even ask each other the questions when we used negative statements. This practice really helped us both become clear about what we wanted so we could focus on our wants, not on what we didn't want.

To finish this story, I decided that what I did want was a job that let me use my creativity, while working Monday through Friday with holidays off. I wanted to make $10,000 more than my last job, and I wanted to work within a fifteen-minute drive from my home. I took small steps and dedicated one hour, four days a week to work toward my goal. At times, I worked on my lunch break or 15 minutes before bed; sometimes I even woke up fifteen minutes early. Sometimes I would do a little more, but only when I was inspired and excited to do it. I researched, created a resume from an online template, and started to apply to jobs that fit my criteria. I ended up with a job creating newsletters for a company that I could ride the local bus to, so when I bought a monthly pass, I saved money and eventually saved up for an even newer car. I then used the exact same process to begin exploring how we could purchase our first home, and now we are living there! Each desire didn't happen like magic, and there were several problems we had to solve along the way, but we made it! The best part of all this is that one day, when my daughter was 17, she came to me with a list in her hand. The list contained the requirements that she wanted for her summer job, and she told me that she knew that she could make it happen by using the same process that I used for my new job and our house. She said she knew that if she decided what she really wanted and started taking the little steps to make it happen, it would! Now when I look back, I'm so glad that I was able to help my daughter while helping myself!

They Watch Us Every Day

C.H., Germany

Moms and dads work so hard that we all need to celebrate the big and small wins in our lives. A friend of mine had been working hard to grow a vegetable garden in the lawn behind her apartment. She was so proud when she finally was able to pick her first vegetable from the garden that she shared her excitement with me over a video call. I was explaining to her that she should celebrate her success and all the hard work she put into the garden and always be proud of the big and small wins in her life. I ended by saying that she deserved it! A few days later, I was doing many loads of laundry because I was so far behind. When I folded the last bit of laundry, I made the comment that I was so happy because for the moment, every piece of dirty clothing was clean. My five-year-old didn't skip a beat and replied, "I think you should celebrate your small win; you deserve it!" I looked at her and we laughed and laughed. Then I told her she was right, and we sat down together and planned a fun celebration for the weekend. I was surprised at first, but then I realized that we are role models to our children, and I was happy to help her learn that it's important to take the time to celebrate ourselves.

Balance and Self-Care

M.K., United Arab Emirates

My day usually goes something like this: I bathe my children, dress them up, and give them breakfast, all while I am still in the clothes I slept in. My two-year-old daughter and I count her colorful balls while I feed my newborn son. I need to fold the laundry, sometimes even twice, because it was dumped out by my daughter. When the kids are napping, I also want to take a nap even though it's not noon, but so many things are running in my mind and rest is crucial. It's also true that I won't get to take a proper nap because I have to wash bottles, fold a load of laundry, sweep and vacuum, put toys away, wash dishes, and take a shower.

There are times when I am just in the middle of my work and my newborn son gets up so I have to change his diaper, feed him, burp him, and lay him down to sleep while singing a lullaby.

I totally end up neglecting myself and I don't get to even eat properly. When I am getting ready to eat, I am still unable to as my daughter is up and often some work is left unfinished. I need to change her diaper, put on her favorite poems, and make a snack for her.

At times, I don't even remember if I have eaten yet and it is already time to prepare dinner.

This is what I do every day as a stay-at-home mom. It's a montage of my daily routine and shows that I'm doing my best to keep things that I love balanced.

Being a full-time stay-at-home mom is tough. Sometimes I think that I don't even have enough time for myself. When my babies need me, I have to attend to them whether it is late at night or early in the morning.

I get up with my children and I am never rested enough to feel fresh. I take a shower in a few minutes, and I always keep the door open as I have to keep an eye on both my kids. I have to be alert all the time for any situation to arise. When my husband is on a holiday, everything gets easier for me as he helps me throughout the day.

My story is about the choices that led me to become a stay-at-home mom. I used to be a very passionate Montessori teacher. In 2015, I was enjoying having built a wonderful career. After five years of teaching experience and practice in this field, I knew it was all about educating your child in a right way at a right time.

Guiding, supervising, presentations of hands-on material, and facilitating and assessing students while they are learning in a prepared environment were a part of my main responsibilities. I loved working with kids and was passionate to help them reach their potential.

I am a postgraduate in education, and I had planned to do a PhD next, but it didn't work out. I didn't pursue my studies any further. Instead, I met my future husband and got married. My life changed quite a bit. In 2019, I became a mother and I wondered how I could ace motherhood and become a good influencer for my child. Finally, I decided to stay at home and raise our child, as I wanted to be present for her and never miss her first laugh, crawl, walk, or word.

This was totally my decision, and it took me many months to accept this role. Yes, I did get those nagging doubtful thoughts: *What am I doing? What about my career? My studies will go to waste. How will I manage things financially? My children might not get benefits that other kids do and I will regret this in the future.*

I know a mom is responsible to help her child develop motor, social, emotional, and communication skills while they are at home. I know most of the helpful activities, and whenever I do such activities, both my kids have fun and learn a lot. I try to involve them in our daily life. I try to guide them rather than control them or leave them completely on their own.

Whenever I am busy in the kitchen, my daughter comes and stands beside me. I am used to counting the cups and plates and telling my child the numbers and shapes of the dishes whether it is a circle, square, or rectangle. I teach her to figure out the difference of less or more items and even short or long items. This will help her to learn fast, through activities. I noticed her math is good and I realized this during meal preparation time as it is the best time when I am measuring estimating, comparing, counting, and recognizing shapes.

I love plants and I do some gardening at home sometimes. My son loves it too. I count seeds and start telling parts of the plants and their growth and even how much they need water. This increases my son's knowledge of science.

My daughter learns phrases or different words from me and even tries to copy my accent sometimes. I try my best to always be polite and avoid harsh words in front of my children. They have adopted this habit from me and never argue with other children or adults.

I have done many things to enrich their English vocabulary. We play an "I spy…" game; we do sorting activities, coloring, and tracing together. I also take them outside and explore nature with them.

I know these activities will help them sharpen their minds and build and grow their concentration level. These activities will give them confidence to get out there and take part in exciting adventures and contribute meaningful things to society. This will help them in refining their personal skills, building independence, and feeling self-reliant.

When I chose to be a stay-at-home mom, I was very worried about the responsibility of raising children and how I would stop them from taking in the negatives of this world and instead focus on the positives. But over time, I have learned that my kids will copy my husband and I and will be able to learn from our actions and words. Some learning happens directly but some indirectly. They now understand how to react if something breaks, how to comfort each other if they happen to fight, and how to ask for something without throwing a tantrum. They have learned words, numbers, and shapes and they even know how to distribute their time between mum and dad, as they only see their dad at nights or very early in the morning.

These mannerisms are adopted by them because of what they see my husband and I do. I would say the majority of their time in a day is spent with me. The approach to teaching and learning would be very different if they were older, and I am hoping to also learn as they grow.

I would say the secret to handling motherhood is taking care of you simultaneously. The sad irony is that the moment motherhood starts, it is very hard to take time out for yourself, but that is when you absolutely should. This is not just for you but for your children. We cannot give from an empty cup. If a mother is not happy, healthy, refreshed, and even energetic, she can't give her all to her children. Not only will she suffer, but her kids will also because of the lack of attention. On this note, I hope my children learn time management and self-love and their importance by seeing my life and daily routine.

I believe we always learn when we participate together. My children and I are all gaining benefits as I am teaching my kids, and this will help me to gain more life experience and I can share my knowledge with them. Through this, I can learn more skills and my kids will work on independence and intelligence. It took time but things are under control now. I have learned to stick to my schedule. I do my house chores and my self-care routine while the kids are taking a nap. By setting their routine to put them to bed early, I have really helped all of us.

Now that things are settled and I have the luxury to think about myself, I am working to recognize and polish my chosen skill, and that is writing. I am offering my services online such as lesson planning, articles, and even summary and research writing. I am also learning other skills from online videos. Learning new skills would only help me to create a cozier and more peaceful place for my family to rest and thrive in.

Passing It Down

C.M., Alabama, USA

My story is simple, but it really made me realize how our children learn from us every day. One day my oldest son was upset because he was assigned to be a tour guide for new students at his school. He was nervous about this because he had to practice the script he was supposed to recite when he gave the tours to the new parents and their children. I remembered the part in *The Power of Moms with Dreams* book about building confidence by pointing out similar past achievements and accomplishments. I shared with my son how I was nervous when I had to talk to my coworkers and that thinking back to all the times that I had to speak in front of my class while I was younger helped me realize that I would succeed. We then discussed times in the past when he successfully accomplished something and times that he had been fearful of doing something, such as having to introduce himself at his new school, presenting his science project to his classmates, and memorizing his school lessons. He seemed surprised that I still had similar feelings at my age and felt better after our discussion of how he already overcame other situations with success. The day came when he led the tours, and he felt so proud of himself at the end of the day.

Several weeks later, I heard my two sons having a discussion in their room. My youngest son was upset about a sport tryout that he had the following day. As I started to walk toward their room, I heard my older son echo the same talk that he and I had previously. I stopped in the hall as my son pointed out the many times my youngest son had overcome a similar situation and survived. He even explained how he felt when he had to give the school tours and how proud he was once he started doing them. He told him he actually enjoyed them and felt prouder each time he did one. I could tell by my youngest son's voice that he was calming down and really listening. I was so proud that day because I not only realized that my son learned from something that I said, but that he had experienced it, will remember it, and was helping his younger brother learn from it!

This Is My Dream

S.M., Pakistan

Life is unpredictable. Ups and downs are a part of life. There are never-ending struggles, a lot of bearings and a lot of hurdles one must face. Every woman's success should be an inspiration to another. We're strongest when we cheer together. Every woman is precious and incredible in her way. In life, we all have goals and dreams that we want to achieve. The ones that are on their way to achieve and those who have already done it share one simple secret: they put in the work.

Every story has a history, a strong background, and inspiration. My story is about my struggling mother who never gave up. She started her career at the very early age of 18 while working at a government school as a primary teacher. She was a young girl with many dreams in her eyes. My mom is one of eight siblings. My aunts and uncles were busy studying, but my mother was compassionate and wanted to assist her father with his meager income.

The train of life was going on and on, and one day my father sent a marriage proposal for my mother. After a bit of investigation, my grandfather said yes to the proposal. Like my mother, my father was also a government servant and a self-made person. My mother and father both believed in supporting themselves financially. My mother's sisters married wealthy families, but my mother never expected any financial help from them.

My aunts had their own big houses and cars, but my mother was happy with her life. She remained busy with her career, and she also worked at home. She did things like sewing clothes for others and making soaps and detergents from her home. She also raised hens, cooked, and sold eggs to her colleagues.

It wasn't easy doing all this and raising five children, but she never lost hope. Instead, she became stronger to provide the best for her children. She never came back home without bringing fruit or a meal. She kept up with her chores even though she was lonely and busy with her job. With all that she was doing in her life, she always focused her main goal on educating her children. Like her relatives, who were at high posts, my mother dreamed of making her children prominent officers.

She had a dream of building a home instead of renting her house. She took a loan from a bank that was on a 15-year installment plan. Fifteen years is not a small-time frame. However, she did not lose hope. Even though my mother had siblings that had prestigious careers, she didn't want to rely on anyone else. She wanted to achieve her goals on her own.

One day, the school where she worked was banned by the government. They closed the school in which she had been working at for over 23 years. The government then transferred her to a school very far away. It took her two hours to get there. She would have to wake up at 5:00 am in the morning, prepare breakfast for her five children and their father, then get ready for her trip to the school. Her two-hour trip required the use of three different local buses to finally get to her destination. Even though just traveling to her work was a hectic task, she continued to be hopeful and struggled hard to provide a bright future for her children. She finally began to see some of her hard work pay off when my brother received admission to a private university. She was very happy.

Then one day, my mother got into a severe accident. She suffered extensive injuries and had to be confined to bed as a result. My brother wanted to leave his university so that he could start working to help my mother recover but my mother refused to let him leave his school. She wanted the best for her child and told him to continue his studies. My brother then decided to start a part-time job to help out financially.

Once my mom recovered, she continued her teaching career of over 42 years, and most of all, she succeeded in her mission of providing the opportunity of a wonderful education for her own children. The dedication and desire to succeed and reach her desired goal was a positive force and made her the perfect role model for her children.

All her children excelled. One of her children worked in banking and completed an M.B.A., another is an engineer and completed honors degrees, another is a psychologist, one is a lecturer and position holder, and I have my master's degree in mass communications and have worked in different media channels. I am also a freelance mom!

From This Moment On

S.L., Canada

The first day I held my daughter, I remember thinking, "From this moment, I am going to pursue my goals and dreams because of you, baby girl." Saying it was a struggle to have her is an understatement. She is truly a miracle baby, and I knew from the moment I held her that I wanted to create a better life for her—one where I could own my own business working from home so I could spend more time with her. While pursuing my goals, I realized how much my little girl was picking up along the way. How exactly did pursuing my goals introduce success habits for my little girl? Let me share my story with you!

Before I share my story of how I was able to quit my full-time job in four months, I am going to tell you where it all started. My reason "why" I even started my business was my little girl.

I started my business on maternity leave and was able to quit my full-time job in only four months.

And my reason "why" kept me going! My story starts in February 2016 when my whole world came crashing down. My son, Scott, passed away, and after months of searching for answers, my husband and I finally decided to speak with a fertility specialist. I was told that I was unable to have children and that if I wanted to try, it would cost thousands of dollars for a chance. I didn't accept that answer. After that, it took years to get pregnant and have a healthy pregnancy. I had miscarriage after miscarriage. The doctors were telling me to give up, but all of a sudden I got pregnant with my little girl, who was born healthy January 2018.

The reason I started my business was my little girl. It wasn't always an easy journey for me.

From the moment I held her, I knew right there those dreams were possible. That I could have anything come true because I was holding my little girl—something the doctors told me I couldn't have. From the moment she was born, I wanted to pursue my goals so I could inspire her, to teach her that she can achieve anything she wants and to never give up.

Near the end of my maternity leave, I launched my business as a virtual assistant, getting my first client in my first week! I worked during every nap and night, growing and networking my business. When the end of my maternity leave came, I ended up going back to my full-time job because I wasn't ready to take the risk. This was when I became partners with my friend, Chelsea, and together we grew our business so we both could quit our full-time jobs in only four months! Once Covid hit, our business, CS Planners, launched us to an even higher level and we grew incredibly fast.

I was able to achieve everything I ever wanted, being able to stay home with my daughter while working from home, all because I thought my goals were possible. Did I have people bring me down? Yes, absolutely. But don't ever let anyone bring you down because as Audrey Hepburn said, "Nothing is impossible. The word itself says 'I'm possible.'"

I now look back at my journey and realize how far I have come and how my daughter was able to pick up on everything, even at such a young age. She is such a confident, caring, and determined little girl. I remember when she was 10 months old, she was running around the house screaming in excitement because she was finally able to walk. I watched her fall over and over again, so the moment she was able to fully walk, she was so proud of herself (and so was I of course!). Now at two and a half years old, she turns to me while I am working and says, "I am so proud of you, Mommy," and "I love you, Mommy." It's moments like these when I realize how much it is worth the journey and all the struggles.

I want to be able to inspire other moms to pursue their dreams, because you can do it. Even if you are struggling right now, one day you will look back and it will be part of your story.

LIFE IS SHORT

A.G., Florida

When I was a kid, I remember my mom taking care of us. She cooked, she cleaned, she drove us to school, she helped us with homework—everything. Don't get me wrong, we had a dad, but from my perspective, he was the guy who'd sit at the kitchen table on Sunday morning reading the paper while my mom caught up on the laundry and dishes. I was too young to see the bigger picture, but I did feel that it didn't seem very fair.

The older I got, the more involved my dad became, maybe because older children are easier to handle. They can walk and talk, use the toilet, feed themselves. I was still excluded from the fun trips he and my brother would take though. I figured they assumed a girl wouldn't want to go camping or go watch the races. That wasn't true. I think it would've been fun to experience those things with my dad and brother as a kid, but I was never invited.

Even when I was a little older, I was never asked to go. I never invited myself, and I loved having one-on-one time with my mom, but I have to admit that it did make me resent my dad a little.

Of course, he provided income for the family, but the funny thing about that was they both worked full-time jobs. She brought home just as much money, and she still managed to maintain our whole household. She approached cooking, cleaning, grocery shopping, sports, holidays, and Sunday dinner at my grandmother's house all with a smile on her face.

As the years went on, her smile began to fade though. It always seemed bright to me, when I was young and naive and all I ever felt was love from her, so I didn't know any better. There was a coldness rolling in though, and I could tell at night, when the house was silent and I'd hear my parents quietly bickering in the other room. Sometimes I'd even go to my brother's room so I could watch TV with him; otherwise, I'd find myself eavesdropping.

One day my dad sat us down at the table with my brother and me, and he began to cry as he told us our mother had filed for divorce. I was alarmed. It caught me off guard, especially because my dad was not very emotional. He didn't want her to go. He didn't want us to go, but it was too late.

Their divorce was anything but cordial, my brother and I being shuffled between two homes, walking on eggshells, and getting used to this different life. It was awkward at first, but once school started back up, it turned into a normal routine.

My mom ended up meeting a man she fell in love with—a man I was more than happy to welcome into our lives and beyond proud to call my stepdad. A man who spent time with me, played outside with us, took us to see movies, cooked me dinner, cooked my mom dinner, asked her how her day was, and dropped everything to help her if he noticed she needed it. That was the type of energy a woman like my mom deserved, because that's the type of energy she gave, and she met someone who was ecstatic to return it.

We moved out of our old family home and into a new house that they built together, where they merged their lives. It wasn't long before they decided to get married. They held a cute little wedding for their friends and family in the backyard of our new home, and I remember it being such a lively party—a Hawaiian luau-themed fiesta that I still revert to when I need a humbling memory.

I say that because ten days later, my mom passed away. She had been diagnosed with cancer the previous year and continued to fight for as long as she could. She didn't have enough time to enjoy all that she worked for and all that she deserved, but she taught me a lifetime of lessons.

I learned a very valuable lesson from watching my mom take control of her life again, and that lesson will impact my life and stick with me forever. In a time when divorce was frowned upon, she decided to stand up for herself and let the world know that she deserved a better life. Unfortunately, I also had to learn that life is too short, and to take those chances sooner than later, because they may not always be there tomorrow.

Journey from Low Confidence to Success

S.F., Pakistan

I believe that although it is not easy to do certain things in life, it is not impossible. Here's my story. Twenty-five years ago, my life was in turmoil. When I would go to a function or apply for any type of job, I faced body shaming. Due to this, I suffered greatly and had many difficulties regarding my career. Although this was happening to me, I did not give up. I continued my struggle and hard work, even when it took me a long time to succeed.

During that time, I went through many troubles, but I kept pushing through. It had been over 10 years since I got married, but things did not change and I continued to face difficulties. Even my husband started to say things to me about my failure in my career. We were living a below-average life, and I had nothing to do.

That's when I decided to defeat my failure and silence people. I had to convince myself to get started and not to stop until I had reached my goal. So, I started working hard with determination. Although it wasn't easy, I persevered and continued my efforts.

As I started my journey, first, I divided my work into smaller parts. I understood the value of dividing work into chunks, then making a chart by arranging tasks according to the priority I need to do first. I became in tune with myself.

I paid attention to all the factors, like my body language, verbal communication, look, confidence level, and most importantly, my skills.

It took me five years to reach that goal. When I started, I thought it would take too much time, but I realized the value when I started to observe changes in my growing daughter.

Even though she was very young, she knew all the circumstances and observed everything deeply. She was noticing the steps that I took to alleviate my problem.

I started home exercises and joined a gym to reduce my weight and improve my outlook. I would get up early in the morning, at five o'clock sharp, and start my household chores. I discovered that I needed to manage things to prove to myself that I was strong enough to accomplish my goal and remove the tag of laziness.

I worked for 12 hours a day to build my desired career, spent 2 hours in the gym, continued household chores, and learned everything I could to help me succeed.

I never compromised on my efforts and always told myself, "Be strong. You can do it."

In five years, I had built my successful career as a motivational speaker and well-known counselor. I achieved my five-year goal and never looked back. I am now changing the lives of people who were like I once was, victims of negative feedback, and I'm still going strong!

My daughter learned a lot from my experience, and at 10 years of age, she displayed confidence and was a leading student in her school.

My daughter never gives up and handles every situation with strong beliefs and mature decisions.

It delights me when I hear her echo the same words I would always say as I strived toward my goal, "You can do it."

Now I have a strong daughter, a reflection of my five years of efforts and confidence. As I write this, she is 20 years old, freelancing, and practicing as a clinical psychologist (conducting online counseling sessions) and working with NGOs. I am so proud of both of us!

All the Love in Her Heart

J.N., Venezuela

I was only 13 years old when I experienced a sudden and monumental but discreet change in my life. At the moment, I didn't think too much of it; I barely noticed it at first. But the truth is that since then, there was an irreversible change in the way I lived my life, in the way I saw myself, and in the way I saw my mother.

So, I started paying more attention to the daily life of my dear mother, who is, as of today, physically absent. She inspired me in silence. I admired her displays of love, dedication, confidence, and resilience. For a child, however, it can be easy to forget that mothers have a life. They are just as human and vulnerable and sensitive, but they learn how to balance all of it in the most impressive ways. Without flinching, she enjoyed caring for and providing tenderness, protection, and attention for us, her children.

My mother had seven children, a number that if I think too much about, I feel dizzy trying to figure out how she managed it. If you pardon the comparison, we were like puppies, always thirsty for love and shelter and so much attention. That's how my mother started keeping in her chest her wishes and dreams. She sacrificed so much for us. Back then, it was her only choice. But, as I grew older and we started talking more openly with each other, she was quick to reassure me that she persevered in many different ways. Just as rewarding as pursuing any other goal, she became a better person and she was proud of that.

My mother shared her story with me many times, and her words are so clear in my mind. Her successes and her experiences were engraved in my mind as a child at that time. She used to say, "I never had the love of a mother or a biological father. I lacked a hug, a kiss, a consolation, a friendship, or a simple gift. I grew up among the rivers and the mountains and the flowers, before all these buildings and roads and houses. But one day, I was in the company of my friends, the stars, and I said to myself, 'I will give all the love that is in my heart and in my soul to the child or children that God and life want to give me. I will give away my entire heart, and all the hugs, the kisses, and the pampering that I missed so that my children will be the authors of their own story and will be able to create a story better than mine.' "

That is the great truth about life and the love of a mother. It is so inspiring in any circumstance or moment, that even when she felt she was given little in life, she was able to give so much and wasn't resentful. Today, I recognize that I am who I am because of my mother. I grew up with so much love in my life, even if she lived the opposite childhood. But she transformed her pain into the love that made me who I am. I too am the expression of everything she gave me, from the most tender kiss, the briefest prayer, and the simplest dress made with her own hands, to the most powerful hug of consolation that I have received, the most sublime caress, the most significant word I heard—love. It really is all about love, inspiration, and example. That is what my mother gave me, and that is what my daughter receives today. She shares and confirms what I tell today in these lines. Courage, sacrifice, and selflessness are above the discomforts of life that we might face. But we must always move with a hopeful vision and perseverance. We must believe that tomorrow will be better and that dreams are worth chasing. My mother taught me the importance of never giving up faith, never silencing the feelings in my heart, and listening to the faith in the God she taught me to love, and the faith in myself to achieve all my goals. And, above all, she taught me to know that life is not always easy, but a rough start doesn't mean it'll always be like that.

When I talk about my mother inspiring me, a very particular experience stands out from the rest. This was the toughest moment for my entire family, and she showed us the greatest display of courage and strength inspired by love. On this occasion, one of her children's lives depended on the other. My brother needed a kidney transplant, and another one of my brothers was there for him, but the complications were plenty, life-threatening, and bigger than any of us could handle. My mother turned that moment into an inspiring example, where she showed what real love, faith, patience, and physical and emotional strength looked like. She endured the fear and stress and terror of the situation much better than anybody else. She proved to us that everything can be achieved, even the most unlikely of miracles, and that human beings have their innate courage but that you have to know from the purest of feelings how to face your fears. She showed us that you should never look back, you always have to look ahead with the certainty that you can always succeed.

There was that moment when my mother made a promise to her friends, the stars in the sky. This day, with two of her children hanging between life and death, she fulfilled her promise and she gave everything she had to stand by her children who shared an organ so they could continue with their lives. It was at that moment when I told myself that my mother is the greatest source of inspiration and fortitude and courage in the world. It was then where she quietly, without showing weakness, believed in what she promised that day so many years ago, and it was the love and valor with which she taught us to face life that came out gracefully through her. The result was that she guided her two healthy children through the front door and toward the rest of their lives.

During that experience, my mother's example was clearer than ever before. She stood firm with her belief in the God she loved and with the values that she gave us that day, so that they could be our source and tools to achieve the greatest dreams. We learned how to use love, constancy, and loyalty to what we appreciate in life, and thus love dried our tears and showed us all who stood there those terrible days, full of fear and sadness, that above all, we must be strong and believers at heart. This way we will overcome any difficulty like the one that she had at that time, and thus with the shortcomings that she had since her childhood, she taught me and my brothers that we can, like her, achieve everything we want, if we do everything with faith and determination, and without doubts about true love.

This is one of the many experiences in the life of my mother that has filled me the most with inspiration. She left me with the certainty that you must live your life, and fill it with love from within to grow big and always be better people, better children, better parents. No matter what you are given, you can always offer something better.

Today, I am confident my daughter knows who was my first and great inspiration for love. My daughter shared a lot with my mother, and today she shares with me the lessons I learned from my mother. We always move forward, without fear, and forever growing. This is all I inherited from my mother and now share with my daughter. This is my version of a transcendental story that all mothers share. So, I share my story with those mothers that might relate to it in any way, or might learn something new from it.

I hope this story inspires you. Maybe you can listen more closely to your mother, maybe you still have time to share your story with your children. I hope this story inspires you to let go and try to be happier. I hope you let go of the experiences that hurt you, of the things you missed, of everything that you didn't get to have. Instead, as a mother, have the courage and the strength to be different, to offer an abundance of love now that it's your turn. Be an overflowing source of love, and you will inspire your loved ones near or far with your actions.

At the end of the day, all I can offer are my words and a small story that doesn't compare with the indescribable love I received from my mother. But her story and her lessons will live in my heart forever. As a daughter, a mother, and a woman, I'm proud of everything my mother taught me, and one day, it'll be my daughter who will share her story, and our love, gratitude, and pride will live on and on.

A Resilient Spirit

S.O., Missouri, USA

When I moved to the United States, I never envisioned the life I have today. I had never imagined myself to be in the line of business that I have started, and even more, I never envisioned the rapid growth the business has had. I had thought I would be in a career and did not even think I would have a child by now. My dreams were so different from my reality today.

Despite my dreams, I never had a lot of luck career wise. I could never understand why and will not dwell on that. I am a person who has always had a strong determination. I do not give up very easily on anything I set my heart out to do. I give the best I can to whatever tasks are set for me, and I will only quit when there is no foreseeable outcome (which is rare, to be honest). Before I started my business or even took to social media with the aim of turning it into a potential stream of income, I had missed a job opportunity in a way that left me totally heartbroken and shattered. It felt as though a lover abruptly broke my heart. I did not understand at all how I had travelled eight hours with my toddler for a job, and on the day of the interview, it was something as silly as traffic on the road that made me arrive 20 minutes late. The hiring manager did not care what I had to say; they were very dismissive and asked me to reschedule and never took my calls when I did try to reschedule. I was shattered! This was the breaking point for me, and I knew I never wanted to be in such a position ever again. It was at this point I "gave up" on job hunting and decided to channel my inner creativity.

My child is still young (a toddler), but I teach him through my actions to be hardworking and resilient. Resilience will help him thrive in our world today. I want him to live a life filled with purpose and to enjoy his life to the fullest doing what he loves. I want to show him daily what it is to be passionate about what you do and how that translates directly to never working a day in your life. I am not quite there yet, but I already get that feeling where I am working so hard, yet I do not realize it because I love it so much.

So far, one thing I can see in my little toddler is his ability to bounce back quickly from an unpleasant situation. Sometimes it is when he falls and gets up and just keeps going like nothing happened; sometimes it is when he wants something and cries but when he sees he is not getting it, he finds something else to entertain himself with. I already see a resilient spirit in him, and I know I must be doing something right.

Moving Forward Together

A.K., Nigeria

While I may never know the reason my dad treated us the way he did, what I am very sure of is that my mother's courage and her love for me still inspire me today.

I grew up with a physically and emotionally abusive father, and every day, I woke up to him having new and creative ways of how he would make things hard for mom and me. My mom pretty much carried all the responsibilities in the house, while he did nothing but stay at home, drink, and spend her money wastefully. He would beat her at every slight chance he got and most times caused injury. The hatred I had for my dad grew every day as I watched him do those terrible things to my mother.

By the time I was twelve, I was traumatized. I failed in school and had no friends. Everyone basically isolated and ignored me because I was "weird." I was facing a lot in school and worse at home. I wished my dad would change, or better still, that my mum would leave him.

One fateful morning, I woke up to a loud noise that filled the air. "This feels familiar," I said to myself. I struggled to get up from bed while heading for the stairs.

The noise came from the dining room. I stood behind the door and listened to my parents scream at each other. Soon, I heard him slap my mum and throw in some punches. I fell to the floor and shed uncontrollable tears as I couldn't do anything else.

It seemed that was the last straw that broke the camel's back. My mum packed her boxes, picked me up, and we traveled back to the village to stay with her mum, my grandmother.

She welcomed her with open arms and they both shed tears. I saw the pain in my grandmother's eyes as she saw all the marks and scars my mum had over the years, and this was the beginning of life without my father.

I would have nightmares that he came looking for us. I'd wake up from them and scream and my mum would hold me close and tell me that everything would be alright. Well, it wasn't—at least at that time it wasn't. I began to wonder if that was what my life was destined for, pain and chaos. I couldn't go to school, make new friends, or even trust anymore. I was traumatized, disturbed, and wanted to be alone forever. I would cry every day and wish there was meaning to my life. My mum on the other hand had no job whatsoever as she wasn't an entrepreneur but had worked under someone back in the city. She decided that she wasn't going to sit at home and do nothing. I was pretty sure she made that decision for me because she was unhappy about how the past had made me feel and become, and she wanted to change that.

She soon started following my grandmother to her farm where they'd cultivate her land, plant crops, and harvest ripe ones to be taken to the marketplace for sale. Soon enough, she was making decent money from selling food crops in the market, and also going from house to house soliciting for house chores that could fetch her some money.

I saw my mum gradually moving on with life, and I was triggered by that. I was triggered by the fact that she wasn't brooding like I was and seeking revenge. I wanted her to. I wanted her to get closure for all the things that had happened to her. I wanted him to pay for all the pains, injuries, and scars that he had inflicted on her. But she was doing nothing of the sort. My mother continued working and seemed to be doing great, while I kept having nightmares and running to her for comfort. I was battling with a lot inside, and I was slowly dying. I didn't like how I felt.

When I was fifteen, I wrote a long letter addressed to my father, telling him exactly how I felt about him. That he was a failure and a coward. Although, he wouldn't see it, I just needed to make myself feel good. Sometimes when I remember those terrible times, I would be even angrier that she chose to stay with an abuser for a very long time even when she had an option of moving away to stay with my grandma.

As time went on, I asked her a lot of questions, mostly why she stayed back for the damage to get worse and why she wasn't angry anymore. Mom was of the generation that believed in staying in such a marriage just because of the children. She didn't want me to be without a father. But I think I would have been better off with an absent father. "So why aren't you angry anymore? You seem to be happy that he hurt you, and you are taking it very well," I said to her. My mother's reply was one I will never forget.

"I haven't forgotten everything that he did to me, but I have chosen to forgive him so that I can move on. He did the damage, but if I hold it forever, I will cause bitterness to myself and it in turn will hurt me. Stop punishing yourself. Let's move on for our sake. We are not alone, for we have each other."

I held onto those words and wrote them in the tablet of my heart. I cried after that moment we had, and I made that decision to do as she had told me. I started working towards it and made sure that I wasn't brooding, sitting alone, or talking by myself.

I would wake up every morning, go with my mum to the farm, and assist her with all she needed. If the need to leave for the market arose, I would definitely go with her. I would run errands for her and helped her with outsourcing jobs. I would always play with the other kids outside, and I was finally making friends who were my age, and no one thought I was weird or different. I was finally fitting in.

I would still wake up to nightmares of my dad beating my mum or looking for us. I was a bit troubled about those nightmares. I had thought I moved on and wondered what my mum did that I wasn't doing. I was still punishing myself, and I hated that feeling. I wanted to be free—free from the trauma, free from the pain. I wanted those nightmares to stop. I wanted to be at peace again. I decided to focus on other things. I would think of the people around me and also count the positive things that had happened to us and thank God that we weren't dead. A few times I would suddenly remember that I had forgotten about my traumatic experiences because I had focused my mind on the positive things.

Later I resumed schooling. The school wasn't as big and fancy as the one I had attended in the city, but it was perfect. My mum did that for me. She never relented. She gave me all she had, and I was grateful for that. I was inspired by resiliency, and that helped me search for menial jobs that a sixteen-year-old could do and get paid. I wanted to take responsibility; I wanted to ease her. If I also made money, I would be able to cater for some of my needs and wouldn't burden her with a lot of expenses.

A few years down the line, my mum met a widower and they soon started dating. I was happy but scared. I wondered why she wasn't scared of falling in love again. I wondered what it would be like having a stepfather and step siblings. I imagined that we would have differences and fight all the time. But I know my mum—her past will never stop her. And I learned that from her and trusted her. They soon got married and we left the village for the city.

My mother was so many things to me. Not only did she teach me to forget my past to forgive and move on, but she also rekindled my fate in love. My step siblings learned about us and our past and soon loved my mother, our mother. She taught us to be just like her; she inspired us. We all grew up and went our separate ways to fulfill our purposes. I went to one of the best universities in my country, and one of my stepbrothers got a job and the other became happily married. My mother is my unsung hero, my inspiration.

No Longer Weighted Down

T.R., The United Kingdom

For most of us, life can be a struggle at times, especially when you are overweight. If you ask different people why they want to lose weight, they will have one or two reasons to give. While some will aim to stop using food as a coping mechanism for emotional struggles, what motivated me to set out to lose weight and stick with it was that I wanted to fight for the life I wanted.

My weight loss story is proof that anything is achievable when you start loving yourself more. I grew up in a family where food was always at the center of our attention. Coming from an African family, one of the ways my mother expressed her love was by preparing delectable meals for us, which ignited my love for food. I used to buy a whole pizza box and eat it all by myself, so quickly that no one would notice, and then hide the box beneath my bed. As a child, I was fairly active and I enjoyed dancing, which helped me with my weight. But as time went on, my eating habits led me to reach 285 pounds when I was 18 years old. I thought it was just a number and continued my habits. I struggled through high school with my weight as the number on the scales crept up. When I moved to university, I stopped thinking about my health as much. I had independence, which meant I could do whatever I liked and be responsible for it. I had absolute control over what I ate, how I ate, and when I ate it. I did not feel bad about feeding myself obscene amounts of food. I would go out with friends and eat all manners of fast food. I never actually took my health seriously or was consistent with exercise classes. My overall health took a back seat, and being overweight was something I was not ready to address at the time.

My turning point came when I began to receive insensitive and unsolicited comments, especially from people I didn't know. For instance, there was a time one boy called me a hippopotamus at the pool in front of many people. I will never forget that day, as it was a horrific experience. I went home and cried a lot. As of this point, I was already wearing a 42-centimeter waist in men's denim. I cannot even recount all the judgmental stares I received due to my weight. I felt like I had hit the end of the road, so trying to lose weight became an area of concern for me.

When you are overweight, your mental health suffers as much as your physical health. My excess weight controlled my life. I realized I couldn't participate in the activities I used to enjoy. I had always enjoyed dancing, but I did not have the guts to enter any competitions. My confidence levels began to take a back seat, and I struggled with feelings of loneliness and poor self-esteem. For me, it was a pain that almost cost me everything.

I knew I needed to start working on myself to change my lifestyle and to get my life back on track. One week, I would try a weird new weight loss supplement and another, some special fat-burning exercises. I cannot count the different meal plans I tried. I hated every minute of it, and those feelings made it extremely difficult for me to achieve weight loss. It was like I was putting in so much effort but ended up getting into more trouble. I just couldn't take it anymore. At one point, I even decided to stop worrying about being skinny and instead focus only on being healthy and going wherever my body decided to lead me.

I was at my heaviest, 320 pounds at age 21. I got a job as a shop assistant in a grocery store. I would wake up in the morning depressed, not wanting to get out of bed. And when I finally did, I would drag myself to work through the busy, stressful commutes and then force my way through a long, exhausting day. Most times, when I got home from work, I would feel too tired and depressed to do anything worthwhile, so I would crash in front of the TV, where I was constantly exposed to advertising.

I was extremely frustrated, and life was already difficult for me. There were times I had to say no to social gatherings as I constantly felt others would make fun of me or judge me due to my excess weight. Even when I was alone at the park, I would rather sit on the bench in a corner and watch than participate in any game. My stomach was also not helping the matter, as the fat never seemed to go away despite my efforts with exercise and diet.

One day, I decided enough was enough. I was fed up with not being able to do the things I enjoyed. I wanted to be able to go hiking with my friends without having to stop every ten minutes. I wanted to be able to ride theme park rides rather than being told that I couldn't fit in the seat after spending about two hours in the queue. I wanted to be able to travel anywhere without worrying about fitting into an airplane seat or using a seat belt extender. I decided this was not the kind of life I wanted for myself, and I had to make a change.

I began to wonder if there was a simple trick that could turn everything around—a trick that would give me a new lease on life and help me regain my lost self-confidence. So, I decided to lose the weight again, but this time using a different approach.

The hardest part is getting started, but small steps can lead to amazing results. Because of how much weight I thought I needed to lose, I thought I needed to make a significant adjustment in my diet or go to the gym for two hours daily. In reality, it was about setting small, attainable goals and working towards them.

My transformation started from my refrigerator. I went through my fridge, looked at the nutrition labels on all my foods, and began throwing out foods that did not fit my new eating style. I started my own research and watched some recommended motivational videos on social media platforms. They really helped me because there were times that I thought, "I can't do this; it is too hard." I was also inspired to keep going even by the motivational stories of people I read on social media platforms.

And just like that—boom, it happened!

My weight dropped to 241 pounds in December 2017. I could not believe what I had achieved without setting foot in a gym, without undergoing any surgery, without taking drugs or supplements, and without engaging in any strenuous activity. Instead of tracking and counting calories, I only ate when I was hungry and only until I was satisfied. I went for a short walk daily to keep myself active. I reached my target weight of 135 pounds after 16 months of hard work!

I was without a date all through those periods I was overweight. Of course, I thought, who would want to date someone who looks heavy like me? Now I began to look awesome! I started a relationship a few years ago. It was my first relationship, and after about nine months, my boyfriend asked me to marry him. It was such an incredible feeling to be able to say, "Yes, I will marry you!" Because of my weight loss, my kids are used to hearing yes more from me, whether to go on a vacation, camping, or to the park. I am now the mom I wanted to be, with no limitation and no fear of body shaming whatsoever, and my children have a real-life example of how to achieve their goals by consistently taking one small step at a time.

Sometimes when I compare how I looked many years ago to how I presently look, I just can't stop laughing. Even though I will be 45 years old in November, my body is the best it has been in my entire adult life. I'm so proud! I now have the confidence that I never had before, and I am living my best life.

My biggest lifestyle change came from discovering the life I wanted for myself, and not only did it help me, but it impacted my children. I like to tell people who have just embarked on a weight loss journey to create their individual world and to be happy. They should not force themselves to do something they do not enjoy doing, but to find something they enjoy doing to help them get active. It is easy to include exercise and healthy food into a daily routine without having to set aside a dedicated time for exercise. I believe this is a great way to get started, and I'm glad that I did for me. I am now a role model for my children.

Meeting to Remember

N.S., Dominican Republic

I must start this anecdote by mentioning that as of this writing, I am twenty-two years old and recently graduated (it has been less than a year since my graduation) from the most prestigious university of my country, the Dominican Republic, as a civil engineer. I minored in project management. Even though I only recently graduated, I do have some experience in the field. During my college years, I did an internship of four months as a resident engineer in the construction of an important office building of a renowned company in my country. Besides the already mentioned, I must add to my academic preparation the fact that I can speak Spanish and English perfectly. Contrary to what could be believed, I have spent three months trying to get a job as a civil engineer, but it has been a failed mission. Previously, I was working in a small construction company, where I lasted only three months and decided to quit. I had a much less than decent salary, I was quickly losing weight because of the strenuous working hours, and if I had continued these conditions any longer, I have no doubt health problems would have started emerging. I was forced to decide between my health and the job. For the sake of my well-being, I made the decision to let it go. I quit the job, hoping to get something better, with adequate pay and a schedule that respects the fact that I need time for myself and is healthier for me. I have to say that the job searching task has been much more complicated than I thought it would be. Companies demand years of experience that I cannot get if I am not given the opportunity. It is a great struggle that I have had to deal with, and it seems unbelievable to me that despite my preparation and my abilities, I must struggle with this.

In the midst of frustration with my work situation, I started having negative thoughts. For example, the feeling that I was not enough, that I was not good, that I had made the wrong career choice, and many other things like the ones mentioned before. At times, these thoughts used to get even worse. I say all this because, in the middle of my existential gap, it was one of these thoughts that led me to reflect on my way of seeing things. The thought I am talking about refers to being tired, bored, and disappointed with life itself. The same way I used to think this to myself, I talked about it: I told my mother about my thoughts. At the time we talked about it, I explained to her how frustrated and stagnant I felt. Among the many things I said, I mentioned a phrase that left her dumbfounded, because now I understand that they are very strong words: "I am tired of life." She opened her eyes in complete surprise, but she did not say much. However, in the evening, when all my relatives were in the house, she decided to host a meeting. My mother went room by room to tell my siblings and me that we were going to meet at the dinner table. At the time, my brothers and I were surprised, as we had never been through anything similar. In fact, we tried to just ignore that meeting call, but my mother insisted until she had us all seated together in the dining room. Once we were all together, my mother told us that she would give us a little talk because she had heard a comment from one of us that deserved immediate attention. She began her talk by asking each one of us, "How are you?" To which my older brother replied "fine," my younger brother said "so-so," and I said, "not well." After I answered, my mother proceeded to ask me four questions: 1) Are you healthy? 2) Do you have a roof over your head? 3) Do you get to eat well every day? 4) Were you lucky enough to have access to a good education? All the questions were answered with a yes. At that moment, she began to make me see a reality of life: There are many people suffering from health issues, many others do not have a roof to spend the night under, some lack food or basic resources to survive, and few in our country are those who have the possibility of completing a higher education. Taking into account the above mentioned, which can be said to be the most basic and important things in life, I can say that I am doing well. I have to say that after hearing these words, my mentality was immediately renewed. I started to see things in a different way, to think that I should be much more grateful for what I have and to fight with a positive mindset for the things I want to achieve. But the talk did not end here.

After talking about the aforementioned, my mother then touched a somewhat unexpected topic. She began to tell us about her past. She told us specifically about her childhood, the fact that she grew up in the first years of her life with comfort and a family with stability, because her father had gone to the United States to work, in search of the typical American dream so desired by Latinos. Thanks to this, my mom, her siblings, and my grandmother lived well (because my grandfather was doing excellent abroad and my grandmother also had a job). My mom, my uncles, and my aunts had the opportunity to study in very good private schools, wear good clothes, and always have food, among many other comforts. However, a few years after my grandfather left the country, he stopped providing for the family, and since his contribution was very important for the family, everything went downhill when they stopped receiving it. This way, they went from having everything to having practically nothing. My grandmother had to start working two jobs. She had to work hard for little pay. She had to do all kinds of honest work in order to cover the basic needs of her home, because she had to support and raise seven children by herself. That is how things went in the family, until my mother and siblings grew up and were able to work, help around the house, and improve the situation. My mother told us that the reason she was telling us this was so that we would understand that, in life, we go through good and bad times. Not everything is rosy. Not everything is positive and good, but from everything, we can learn something that will help us grow as people. She told us that bad times do not last forever, that they should be taken as life lessons, and that we should fight in an honest way to improve the areas with which we are not happy.

Continuing with the meeting, my mother went on to talk about when she was already in her youth or early adulthood, when she also had struggles, but already at that stage of her life, the struggle to keep values intact was stronger than in her childhood and adolescence. My mother re-emphasized that she was not a person with great comforts as she is today; she lived simply with basic necessities. She specifically mentioned that she on many occasions looked at how some of the young people around her would walk around the streets of the town where she lived, with expensive clothes, high-end cell phones, among other things, strutting around with money obtained thanks to illicit businesses. However, she was very clear when she mentioned to us that despite seeing these kinds of things, she did not despair. She told us that she could have entered that world to get money quickly, but what comes easily goes away easily. With sadness in her eyes, she told us that today, many of those people are in jail, dead, or struggling with their mental wellness, because of the life they were living. She said there are things that give you momentary happiness but ruin your life forever, tarnish your reputation, and end the tranquility of not only yours, but of all your family members. It was very nice and exciting to hear my mom say that, thanks to her perseverance, today she is well, healthy, and lives life with a clear conscience, without fear of persecution. She is a person who has struggled a lot and therefore knows how to value material goods, but more important than that, she knows how indispensable and necessary values and principles are in the life cycle of a human being. My mother is the hardest working person I know, and today, she has a law degree. My mother emphasized that each person has their own life clock, and we have to work hard to achieve what we want, our goals or dreams, but we must also keep in mind that we must be patient, because good things often take time. She told us that it is very important not to compare or compete with other people, that we have to be focused on our own path.

After listening to everything my mom had to say, without a doubt a change happened in me. Today, I am a different and improved human being. I take my free time to grow as a person, improve my qualities, study, and learn new things that help me to be closer to my goals. I thank her very much for accompanying me and guiding me, even in my darkest moments.

Never Give Up

T.A., Pakistan

I still remember the day when I was sitting before my mother crying. She was observing me as I sobbed. Despite her uneasiness, she was sitting still and calm. I didn't see anything but my own distress. Finally, my mother couldn't sit there any longer. At that point, she got up and sat close to me and embraced me. She quieted me and affectionately held my hand, and she started to calm me. I stopped crying and began tuning in to my mother. She appeared calm, but I could feel the uneasiness inside her.

My family's financial circumstance was not good. My and my sister's educational expenses were expanding day by day, and the family costs were immense. It was bothering me so much. I wondered how I would handle everything. My mother clarified to me that there's no distinction between a man and a lady. She explained that ladies can do what a man does. My mother started telling me about herself.

When she first became a mother of two children, she suddenly lost her job. That time was very stressful for my mother because at that time, both my father and my mother needed to work to support their children. My mother started doing many jobs at home, like stitching clothes, cooking food, and sending the food out to restaurants. Sometimes, she was paid well for her hard work but sometimes she was not. At that time, my father supported my mother a lot. When he was able, they both took care of their two daughters, and my mother became even busier sewing more clothes. As time went on, my mother's work grew, and she got a job working in a small boutique. Conditions in our home were getting better, and at that same time, my mother found out that she was going to be a mother again. It was a great moment for my parents, but a few days later, my father's health deteriorated, and he was unable to work steadily at his job. It was a difficult time because my sibling and I were so young and needed care too. With my father being ill, my mother applied for a loan from the boutique where she worked at the time because she was in dire need of money. Instead of getting a loan, my mother was told to leave her job. My mother resumed sewing at home. She worked very hard day and night and kept the wheels of our house running. Days went by, but our situation did not change. One day my mother met a woman as she was about to pick me up from school. My mother was waiting outside and looking very sad as she thought about her situation. The woman was watching from afar and then came and sat next to my mother. After saying hello, she told my mother that she was observing her from a distance. She asked if it was ok to inquire as to why she appeared so sad. My mother told her about my father's illness, and my mother became upset. The woman asked her who takes care of the expenses for her household. My mother informed her that she sews clothes and takes care of the house and other expenses. At that time, I came out of school and hugged my mother. I also noticed the woman who was looking at me with a smile. She told my mother that she ran a boutique and was looking for an employee to work for her. She handed her business card to my mother and told her to contact her if she wanted the job.

When my mother came home, she thought many times that she should work in this boutique. But there was no one else to take care of my father and sister. One day, my father's health worsened and my mother had run out of money for his medicine. Luckily, my mother was able to borrow the money from one of her relatives to purchase the medicine for my father. That's when my mother decided to contact the woman she had met at the school about a job at the boutique. The next day, my mother went to her and asked her for the job. The woman not only gave her the job, but she also told her she could do her boutique work from home. My mother worked day and night from home, and the woman was very happy and satisfied with my mother's work.

Conditions in my home began to improve, my father started getting treatment in a good hospital, and in a few days, he started recovering. At the same time, God blessed my mother with a third daughter. My father started to feel better and took great care of my mother. Because of my mother's hard work, she became the manager of that boutique, and my father was able to return to a good job. I looked at my great mother without blinking. I was prouder of my mother than ever before and for myself that I was a daughter of a great mother who struggled so hard for her daughters and home.

Fast forward and once again, the test of our destiny had begun. By now, my father had retired, and my mother was also no longer working. Our family had grown to include four sisters. I was now older and it was my turn to be as brave as my mother was and to seek employment so that I could bring happiness and peace to my dwelling like my mother had. I made the decision to not give up and to move forward with determination, just like my mother. I got up one morning and my mother looked at me happily and asked, "Where are you going?" I looked at my mother and said, "I am going to explore this world so that I can bring you back the same peace and happiness that you gave to us." My mother's face lit up with joy as she saw the determination in my eyes.

I started looking for a job and came back every day frustrated. My mother encouraged me a lot. I also had to pay for my studies. I had to take a course, but I did not have enough money to pay for it. I could barely cover my university expenses. I did all that I could to save money, and even when the other students paid for copies of the class notes provided by the teacher, I took my own notes to save money. My mother encouraged me throughout all my worries.

Finally, as I finished my degree, I was happy that I would now be able to get a good job. I took my resume to the place where I did my internship, and I was sure that I would get the job because my grades were so good. But, when I went there, the manager refused to give me a job and said, "You are a girl, and there is no place for girls in this firm." I didn't understand why the business did not understand the ability of women.

When I returned home, my mother saw me in distress and sat with me silently. Then she reminded me of her story. I didn't want to upset my mother. Looking at my mother, I thought, "My mother never gave up, so neither will I." I told my mother that nothing could stop me. So what if I am a girl? I can do everything. After that day, when my mother comforted me, I started to wake up and began working on my goals. I wrote for newspapers. I continued putting in hard work and dedication. I had tutored in the past, and at that time, I started tutoring again. My online work began, and I am happy to report that I am moving forward with financial success because I did not give up. Presently, I am working as a freelancer and a writer. I am happy with my job and my life! My mother is a role model for me, and every step of the way, she taught me that I can do anything and that I should never give up!

Reborn

A.M., France

The plan seemed clear, to go to France in 2019. It was the perfect opportunity to grow up. We had lived together in Panama since 2018, but the economic situation in the country was becoming difficult, the salaries were very low and the opportunities very few. For a person like me, being a social communicator by profession and specializing in marketing, I wanted more. I've always wanted more. But the unexpected happened, a month and a half delay of menstruation announced what was not included in the plan. A baby was on the way, and everything we had planned completely changed.

The trip to France was still on, but in this case, we decided I would no longer look for a job, but would instead focus on something more important, our child. Meanwhile my partner focused on work to help our growing family.

When we arrived in France, the first month was incredible because I was discovering my new country. I had already visited France for vacations, but this time it was going to be my home. After that month of exploration, reality hit hard. I lived moments of great loneliness, anguish, and then something I wasn't familiar with came to my door: anxiety. Every day it was worse; being in a country where I didn't speak the language, expecting a baby and being far from my family was challenging.

Even though my partner's family was French, it wasn't the same, it would never be the same, and I continued to feel that way throughout my pregnancy. The day our baby arrived brought even more anxiety. I had a complication in childbirth that almost ended my life, a complication millions of mothers in the world die from. I had a hemorrhage of more than two liters of blood and it was at that moment that I was born again. I can attest that from that moment of so much pain, I have never been the same. Without a doubt, I changed. My innocence and young free spirit died that day and a mother was born. I became a woman who had to be strong without options. It is difficult to fully understand how I felt unless you experience it. No matter how many books and courses you take, I believe that only experience gives you that title.

And that's how I began to forget who I was and my love for my work. The anxiety was much more intense and there are still many things I don't remember. I think my brain suppressed them to protect me. I couldn't say for sure how it happened so quickly, but I really bottomed out.

I knew the term postpartum depression at its best. There I was at three in the morning breastfeeding a newborn child, with no one to take care of me, because now it was ME who had to take care of a small defenseless baby. I started to wonder who takes care of the mothers at that time? I thought it was supposed to be your own mother, but in my case, she was quite far away so I had to fend for myself with strength and courage. My husband was at work all day and I felt the need to be strong for my baby.

My whole family lives in Venezuela, I migrated to Panama when I was 24 years old, I did it alone, full of dreams, wanting to take on the world. I was able to work in marketing agencies and have very rewarding experiences. It was there that I met the father of my daughter, a young French man, who had moved to Panama with his father to open an aluminum company. I lived in that country for five years.

When we were in France and our daughter was two months old, I couldn't take it anymore and decided that I needed to work. My mind was on the verge of collapse because my days were filled with diapers, anxiety and sore breasts. I still didn't speak French, so I had to create a plan B. It was then that I decided to try to look for online work. It was the middle of a pandemic and working online had increased by sixty percent. Luckily, I had already worked online before, so I convinced myself that I needed to do it again, but differently.

I opened an Instagram page specialized in all my knowledge and experiences and by the end of 2020 I already had more than 20 new clients. I helped them with designs for their social networks, web pages and advice. Little by little I felt like me again even though when I looked in the mirror, I didn't even recognize myself. My body was 15 kilos overweight; my hair was messy and I noticed an aura that wasn't shining like it used to. My decision to return to what I loved helped me begin to see the light. I realized that my baby deserved a happy healthy mom and role model.

Today, I continue working online, and traveling all over the world. I've already explored more than 10 countries in Europe and I plan to go for more. I feel full, I am happy, and my daughter is almost 3 years old! She is becoming quite independent and I am so very thankful for her and her father.

I am grateful and happy that I was able to find the perfect balance in my life! Motherhood is not easy, but I can attest that when you are in a country that is not yours and you do not speak the language, the challenges can be even more intense. You need strength and courage to lead yourself in the right direction, but once you look inside and find the balance in your life, you not only achieve wonderful things, but you have so much more to give, including a wonderful lesson to share with your child in the future!

A Life Worth Watching

I.L., California, USA

As some say, history is always bound to repeat itself, but not on my watch. Perhaps I could have become an emotionally absent parent, but I know better not to fall victim to the same faulty programming that my ancestors fell for. We have it in our hands to live a meaningful life and to lead by example.

Future generations are now more privileged to have resources to make them amazing parents. Yes, we may face similar struggles, as did those before us, but I know that we hold the pen in our hands to write the story called *My Life*.

Early on in my young adulthood, I took an oath to never be a parent like the persons who raised me. The verbal, emotional, and physical abuse and the disconnect have done me a great disservice in life, and it took a long journey of healing before I felt ready to be a parent myself. I sought to invest in myself every chance I got. I expanded my mind beyond the limits imposed on me as a young kid learning about the world. I learned to enjoy the little things in life and to quit conforming to the one-size-fits-all concept.

My goal was to stand out and dance to my own tune. Naturally, life stepped in and I lost my way for a minute. From the pressures and expectations to be something I am not for the sake of making a living, to the emotional anguish I endured for following others advise on how to parent, left me lost and confused.

As I sat in my living room this one fine day, feeling sorry for my handful of mistakes, beating myself down for failing at my dream yet again, I looked over at my son and my baby girl. Seeing their beaming smiles made me come to my senses. I am a good enough parent and capable of making the right decisions for my family. I did my best and I am learning as I go. I forgave myself for the past mistakes. I will also not take people's criticism to heart anymore and allow my kids to witness my defeat, nor will I lead by such an example.

The next day, I picked myself up and made a promise to myself that no matter what, I would find the way back, and I did. Seeing me take charge, my children also began shifting their behavior. They witnessed my daily gratitude for the little things. The energy shifted in our home, and we were healthier in every sense of the word. No more monthly visits to the doctor, no more nightmares or panic attacks.

These days, they are much bigger and much more aware of the things I do, say, and display. They empathize with their friends and show care to those in need. We all have adopted a morning ritual on the way to school and always start a day with a happy song to get the positive energy flow going. Things are much lighter and more flowy. We say our affirmations and our gratitude daily, and I am witnessing amazing shifts in the way they behave and look at the world.

I see so much light and potential in them, especially now that they are no longer afraid to try new things or to keep trying when they fail. They have a newfound sense of confidence and pride. Leading by example is the best way to raise and cultivate self-sufficient happy kids. It is an investment toward the greater good in the world. Their compassion, their grit, and their intelligence are of tremendous value to society, and this ripple begins with us parents. As a mom and a transformational life coach, I like to say, be aware of how you show up day to day, because your kids are watching you and aspiring to be you, even if they don't show it. Live a life worth watching and witness true blessing in the making.

Lessons from My Mother

S.M., Pakistan

So, let me share with you some things that I learned from my mother: focus on your goals, try to solve your problems by taking the steps required, try to focus on your dreams while working toward them, always trust in your abilities, and earn your own way.

Now from here, my own story began. I was a very chill and fun-loving girl. Due to being the youngest child, I am the most non-serious sibling of all. Apart from my lack of seriousness at times, I was a bright student who always secured good grades in school and college. After matriculation, I completed my intermediate in computer studies, then moved towards my graduation, and then finally my post-graduation in mass communications.

After completing my studies, I started a job at a reputable news channel and started my career at a news network. After having done that job for over five to six years, I got engaged. I was not satisfied with my parent's decision in selecting my husband because I found my fiancé to be very mature and serious. Then I met someone else, and we fell in love, and we got married. My in-laws did not accept our love marriage.

Finally, I was blessed with a cute baby daughter. She became the center of attention for me. I spent my days and nights giving her all my love and care. My husband and I began falling apart, and after almost 2 years of marriage, he found someone new. This really affected my mental health because I began to feel helpless. I was taking daily medication to help me feel better, and I seemed to have forgotten how to laugh. One day I was on social media and people were discussing the topic of freelancing and how to make income as a freelancer. I hadn't worked on the internet prior to this, but I was familiar with writing articles due to my mass communication studies and my work with a writer who wanted me to re-write his writings. Although the pay was not the greatest, and I worked a lot, I learned from him. Then one day, I took on a job in social media marketing.

Finally, after my two-year struggle following my marriage and my knowledge of freelancing, I was able to focus more on my career. With some savings, I left the home I lived in during my marriage and rented out an apartment for myself and my daughter. I now work all day on my laptop to earn a livelihood while writing articles and blogs and completing data entry projects. This job works well for me because I can work at home, since I am the sole caretaker for my young daughter.

Every day is different, and on some of the more difficult days, I sit up at night, staring out the window wondering, "Oh Allah! Where am I going to go from here?" Right now, I'm not certain where I am going, but I know I am going somewhere and only in the right direction!

My vision involves my daughter. I wish to guide her to be as vital and hard working as my mother taught me to be. I want her to be a well-educated professional in society and to live a positive life. I am raising her to be loving and independent, for this is my dream!

So, my message towards every woman around the world is to be self-made and self-reliant. Never lose hope and trust in yourself. Life tests everyone, and that's ok. Some people face their struggles but never give up. Don't sit for long crying; do not solely rely on another, but rely on yourself. Choose your own way according to your skills, and do not stop dreaming. Just fasten your seat belts and start your journey in a positive sense. Do not forget to pray, and watch your dreams come true!

The Art of Silence

A.D., Philippines

I used to think that I was weak and that drama was a normal part of family life. What with more than one family living in the same household, and living not only with the immediate family but with grandparents, aunts and uncles, and cousins, drama seemed to sprout just about any time, anywhere.

When I was nine years old, my parents separated. I stayed with my grandparents from my father's side where my aunt and her family live. My other aunt and my uncle stayed at that house on a daily basis – early morning before they went to their work and in the afternoon after working. There would always be fights about a variety of things – petty things to serious ones. I was the youngest grandchild, and my aunts and uncle treated me like their sister. They would open up to me and pour out how they felt. I've always loved them all. I didn't take sides. What I always really wanted was for conflicts to end. However, I always listened attentively.

Some people, including me, thought I was being weak at the time because I did not have a strong opinion on most issues. I did not jump at people with opposing beliefs. I always chose to listen and to understand. There were a lot of times when I wished that I was more assertive, outspoken, and opinionated. I even tried to be this way at times, but that just wasn't me.

I always heard people telling me, "You should have spoken up," or, "You should have fought back." But in my experience, raising your voice or talking back in the heat of the moment is never a good idea. By just staying silent, listening, and letting the moment pass, I have avoided bigger problems. After cooling off, I realized how listening is a great tool for fixing misunderstanding or even preventing it from happening.

Now, I have come to realize that listening is one of my best qualities. I recognize its value because as an educator, I know that those who listen can teach and learn at the same time, while those who speak but don't listen only teach. I know that listening is a kind of superpower that not many people have these days. People's attention spans appear shorter and shorter. I believe that someone who listens is quite special. This great skill is a skill that I am so happy to now identify in my own son and modeling this behavior seems to have had a big impact on him as well.

When my son became a youth leader in our church and an active officer or member of different organizations, I was able to observe how he communicates with other members. I saw how he would often be quiet during meetings and other gatherings, and in the end, when he found the right moment, he would speak with wisdom, considering what he heard other members say. He would even ask for opinions when he was unsure of things.

Now, he is a freshman in college, taking psychology. I know that listening will take him to places, not just in his future profession but in all his relationships as well.

All Shall Be Well

M.J., Kenya

In 2003, I discovered a lump on my breast. I tried to not over concentrate on it, but I was constantly checking it to see if it decreased in size. Contrary to my expectations, it grew bigger. It almost doubled in size daily. I went to the doctor and at his recommendation, I decided to go for a breast scan. I was later diagnosed with cancer, and the doctors advised me that the best treatment was to surgically remove my right breast. At that moment it was hard to believe that I actually had cancer, and I could not imagine living my life with just one breast. At that time, I had only one child, who was just eight years of age. Her dad had passed away when she was one year old. In short, she never knew the sweetness of having a dad.

    I continued my journey to the surgeon for the scary breast removal. The operation went as expected, and after I woke up, I realized that my right breast was no longer there. More sadly, shortly after the operation, I received notification that my job was terminated. I had worked as an English literature teacher in a secondary school under contract terms. My hospital bills began piling up as I had a long hospital stay. My future looked dark.

    I started overthinking about death as I worried that I could experience a premature death. I kept thinking about my fatherless child, who was blessed with natural intelligence. She was always at the top of her class, and sometimes featured somewhere in her national exams. Now there she was, with no parents! I could not hold my tears when she kept coming to the hospital where I was admitted, held my hand, prayed with me, and always whispered some inspiring words such as, "Mum, all shall be well, take heart!"

    My surgeon came as he normally did, took some tests and came back with the results. He smiled and said, "Your incisions are healed. Your tests are now negative. Your cancer has not spread to other parts of your body. God loves you, young mom." I was very happy. Before I was released from the hospital, my surgeon advised me to continue with frequent medical appointments. My daughter had already arrived at the hospital. I held her hand, and we left the hospital feeling filled with life. I had to deal with trauma that is associated with my cancer diagnosis and the possibility of my cancer coming back, as well as some side effects associated with the surgery and radiotherapy. I kept thinking hard and deeply about my diagnosis, although I did not directly want to show my fear to my young daughter, who believed her prayers had worked out marvelously.

When I received my hospital bills, I could not believe what I saw. The amount had increased tremendously. Without wasting any time, I withdrew my last hard-earned money, which I had saved for my daughter's education and basic needs, to pay my bills. I also ordered some of my stock, like cows and goats, to be sold to raise more money.

Once I was home, I became more afraid because I was bankrupt and jobless. I had to think very fast about where I could get a new job at least to help with my daughter's basic needs. Luckily, I secured a laundry job where I took home a few dollars per day. It was not much, but my daughter could at least afford something to eat and wear.

But as time went on, I noticed that whenever my daughter was free, she would take my phone and spend hours googling about cancer, survival techniques, and how to become a cancer doctor. After I realized what she was doing, I asked her why she wanted to pursue medicine. My young genius replied that she was greatly encouraged by how I had victoriously fought a deadly disease like cancer, so she wanted to study more about it so that she could treat me if the cancer ever re-occurred. I felt challenged by that reasoning and worried about her possible fears, but she seemed more inspired than fearful. I held her hand as she googled more cancer stories from reputable sites and downloaded cancer survivors' videos and their testimonies. My soul felt inflamed by her undying studies, especially in mathematics and sciences.

It's now many years down the line, and I was so proud to see my only daughter in a graduation gown. She is now a degree holder in medicine and surgery, specializing in the field of cancer. What a dream come true! When I looked at my one breast, I smiled and concluded that this was what had encouraged my little queen to study hard! When my daughter's name was called on graduation day, an energy surged through my body. The air around me felt completely electric. I was bearing clear witness to the accomplishments of my daughter's dreams.

I wiped my tears away from my eyes and eagerly embraced her efforts as she proudly clung to her prestigious university degree. I emotionally congratulated her and hugged her tightly against my one breast. Beneath that physical swell of emotions, I felt a bit of guilt. Her achievement was inspiring, yet at the same time bittersweet. My daughter had no chance to share this glory with her dad. My daughter had no chance to take a picture against a physically complete looking mother, and my hands were rough due to the menial work I had taken on after I lost my teaching job.

Guess what? This was exactly what fueled her sheer efforts to work hard for what she achieved. After my experience, I decided to start writing motivational stories to help other potential ladies who might have a zeal to make it in life. I choose to write stories for anyone feeling discouraged with life and hope to remind them that a closure of one door may lead to the opening of a better door in future.

My illness has always been a point of reference in my daughter's efforts. She told me she would do whatever it takes to see me healthier and happier! Wow, that is the undying spirit of a fighter!

Today, I am healthier and wealthier. My daughter is the talk of the town both online and offline. It's hard to believe that my illness encouraged her that much! May Almighty God see the efforts of other young ladies worldwide and help them victoriously fight their battles. May what seems like a challenge become their source of new faith and new energy in life, and may they always remain focused to do whatever it may take to get a remedy! I am a living testimony that a mother can be the role model of their daughter's success story. My spirits and efforts to fight cancer clearly encouraged my daughter to be a doctor! May the Lord crown the efforts of our children!

In Her I Find Strength

H.P., Arizona, USA

My mother was freshly twenty years old when she became pregnant with me. Within two months, she and my father were dockside, exchanging vows on a windy Saturday afternoon in June, surrounded by equal parts family and red rose petals. But, soon after, her flourishing pregnancy came to an unexpected halt. The level of complications forced her to deliver nine weeks earlier than the due date she'd been counting down, day by day.

She was put under anesthesia over a hundred miles away from home and across state lines at the nearest major hospital. She was filled with an unshakable fear, wondering if her baby would survive and if *she* would survive. By 4 pm, I was brought into the world prematurely. In need of an intense level of care to survive that only the NICU could provide, I was whisked away to an incubator. It would be my new home for the coming months—a stark contrast to the comfort of my mother's womb, which was warm and safe. I could no longer feel and hear her voice around me.

When she awoke from surgery, a plethora of information was thrown at her. Her daughter was born weighing 2 pounds, 1 ounce, and was on life support. My father ended up being the one to name me—a first name they'd both tossed around yet remained undecided upon. He'd also given me the same middle name as my mother, something they hadn't even talked about yet. But it was a gift to share a name with her—particularly one so fitting in its meaning of *reborn*.

My mother was also told that the necessary wound that brought her baby into the world was closed, but a blood clot developed and was yet another risk to her. Though all that mattered was that her daughter survived, it was still a defeating update. It felt as if her body was at war against her. So, another procedure followed, removing the tiny threat of cells that could change everything instantly.

Two months dragged by. My mother went two months without the possibility of bringing her daughter home. Instead, every few days, she and my father trekked the handful of hours northward to that same hospital surrounded by the Atlantic coastline to visit their newborn. She used these trips to provide pumped breastmilk for the staff to feed her baby. It was the least she could do. It was *all* she could do to care for the baby exempt from her arms. She was on the outside looking into her child's growth. With each visit, she noticed something new about her daughter.

On one unexpected day, as she and my father prepared to make another visit, the hospital called. What was worrisome to start eventually left them both in ecstatic disbelief. They were told it was their last trip. They could finally take their baby home with them.

They called all their family members, who resided out of state, and told them the good news—many of them packed up to take a road trip of their own. My mother couldn't shake the excitement and the genuine feeling that her daughter was finally hers. At last, she could be the one to care for her. She was excited to do all the things that new parents take for granted: midnight feedings, long bouts of rocking, and dirty diapers. It was everything she'd been waiting to do but couldn't.

The whirlwind of the birth and the following months exacerbated my parents' protective nature. The typical new-parent worries were on full display but even more heightened. I was still a fraction of what other newborns were when they came into the world. I was fragile both inside and out.

Weeks turned to months, and my mother was catching up on the lost time with me. She had a first-row seat to my growth and development and was eager to keep track of it. She smiled to herself as she wrote down each milestone I surpassed. She and my father eventually decided to move back south to their hometown. The little town nestled between two bodies of water still felt like home, no matter how far they ventured. It was where their parents and siblings resided and made the most sense to be as a newly formed family.

After settling in with their six-month-old, feeling that life could only go upward from there, another strike of rarity hit my mother. What started as a typical headache morphed into an indescribable pain that left her debilitated for a full day, then a week, into multiple weeks. Over-the-counter pain medication didn't dent the ache that radiated through her skull. She had endless questions about how this pain had taken over her entire being. Why was nothing stopping it? How was she supposed to function, let alone care for a baby?

She pushed through the pain, confusion, and sensitivity towards all of her surroundings to care for herself and her daughter. My father worked to provide for us, but it still left a heavy burden on my mother to work through the indescribable pain just to get by-pain that was even questioned by others.

After my mom pressed for answers with many doctor visits, a diagnosis finally came. Encephalitis: an infection of the brain that causes severe swelling. A diagnosis didn't ease the pain she felt, but somehow, giving it a name put her at ease and this horrific illness with such a rapid onset wasn't as mysterious anymore.

Treatment was hit-and-miss and provided no guarantees. She tried everything from high levels of anti-inflammatories to acupuncture to relieve the pain. All that eased it was the passing of more weeks and months. The headaches decreased over time in their duration and severity. But each time one struck, a familiar strain of what-ifs filled her mind. What if it never went away?

Years after the initial onset of encephalitis, bouts of swelling flared up without warning. But my mother didn't let it stop her. She cared for her daughter and husband unwaveringly. She even had the desire to funnel some energy into her education. It had been a while since she cracked open the textbooks, but she desperately wanted a college degree. She wanted to learn about things larger than herself and find a place of belonging that she could call her own, brought to her by no one other than herself. She'd persevered through events that she had never fathomed could arise in life and survived. But she had more to prove.

My mother went on to take classes at the local community college. She chipped away at the degree, night class by night class, even bringing me along to sit with a coloring book in the corner if she had to. Her tenacity was shining through, and she was even asked to take on the role of student ambassador during her time at the college. When she finally walked across the stage, she relished in the hard work it took to accomplish a hefty education milestone and grant herself independence in a future career. She'd blossomed from the fearful young woman struck by rarities into a strong woman who'd surpassed hurdles that she could never have come up with, even if in a tailspin of worst-case scenario. My mother came out on top, despite it all.

Today, I can look back at what my mother endured, still only able to grasp her physical and emotional pain at surface level. But I am in awe of her tenacity and resilience and hope that I can possess a fraction of what she has. Her experiences linger in my mind when I find myself encountering unexpected hurdles. I think of how her only way through those times was to push through them, not just for days and weeks, but for months and years at a time. As an adult, now older than she was during those challenging years, I wish I could hug her younger self. I'd tell her she was doing everything right and that she would make it. I'd ensure her that she was paving a pathway, not only for herself but also for her daughter, all while tackling the hardships that were out of her control.

Though I cannot be a source of comfort for the past version of herself, I can recognize that stem of resilience she gifted me and nurture it. I can remind myself that I am part of her in every sense of the word. I am fortunate enough to have someone so strong and persistent as my mother. Someone who could have crumbled under poor circumstances, but still had sight of the goals she'd crafted for herself and accomplished them. While our battles throughout life differ, I strive to carry at least a spark of the perseverance she upheld with me forever.

FINAL THOUGHTS

From the moment a baby is born and locks eyes with their parent or caregiver, they start to observe the behavior, movements, and actions around them. They're constantly watching. A simple act of care, a cuddle, or a comforting hug is enough to display a great deal of affection and make them feel loved, wanted, and safe.

Although verbal language is one of the main pillars of communication, it is not the only one. Our body speaks, and our actions speak. Many times, as adults, we're often faced with the dilemma of meeting someone whose actions don't quite match with their words, leaving us confused. Why would it be any different for our children? An action speaks more than a thousand words, as they say. If we want our children to learn from us, we must be mindful of our actions.

We start to "form" the adult version of ourselves while we're still children, in the very first years of life. The impact of an adult's actions on a child isn't exclusive to their parents either. Any caregiver, parent, sibling, teacher, and other authority figures who have an essential role in that child's life will also be observed, and their behavior will, just like those of the parent, impact and influence the attentive children who are watching.

That's precisely why I decided to start this project by telling my own story. I found it extremely inspiring how my mother refused to give up after my father's unfortunate accident and how that decision, as well as my mother's positive efforts, made a great impression on me, even into adulthood. My parents' story was the perfect example of the importance of having a mother who focused on the positive, and it only influenced and reinforced my own beliefs. My mother could've spent her days complaining and asking God why he would be so cruel to give her such a heavy burden when she had small children to care for. However, she was a positive influence, setting the tone for her children's childhood. Despite all the difficulty she had to experience, I grew up with happy memories.

Then, once I had my own children, not only did I experience positivity and happiness when thinking about my own childhood, but I also wanted my children to grow up to feel the same. My mother's actions inspired me even as an adult. My mother's story was a perfect example and one of the many stories that led me to realize how important it is to act positively in front of your children and to teach them valuable lessons through actions. I knew words were powerful, but I learned that at times, actions speak much louder. Hopefully, some of the stories that you read in this book also relayed that very important message.

How can a mother be a good inspiration to her children? Beyond motherhood, there is often a woman with her own dreams, hobbies, desires, and wishes. That doesn't magically go away once she has a child. This woman is still very much there, waiting for a bit of space amidst the busy life of a mother, looking for the right moment to emerge again. When this happens, allow it.

Parents who have their own desires can really help their children. Not to mention the fact that they are automatically teaching an essential lesson to their children while they still work on themselves and their dreams. It might sound like the perfect scenario, and that's because it is.

What dreams, you may ask. This can be moving into a new home, just like in our story by the lovely J.N., who observed her mother as she dealt with the death of her father and then watched her mother overcome obstacles and create plans that become a reality. From moving to a new town, renting a new house, slowly buying each piece of furniture, decorating each room, step by step, until that house became their home. Just as her mother had once told her about each of the steps they would need to take to achieve their dreams, she saw them all become true thanks to her mother's efforts, which left a more impactful impression than any hour-long speech about determination could ever have.

But it doesn't need to stop there. Your positive influence on a child doesn't necessarily need to be attached to a material thing. We saw great examples in the story of L.S. who had nothing but happy memories about her childhood and wanted to make sure her children followed the same path. Those memories weren't based around anything in particular, let alone something expensive. Quite on the contrary, her happiest moments were simply spending time with her grandparents, having a pool day, and enjoying their company. When she became a mother, she did the same with her children, and they grew up playing games and having fun with their cousins, building core moments that will accompany them for the rest of their lives.

In several of the stories that you've just read, the mothers were able to live a happy childhood, and they were able to pass it on to their children, but there were also several stories of children who learned wonderful lifelong lessons due to the difficult decisions that their mothers chose to make, and observing their mothers' actions created a lasting impact in their own lives.

Please, also understand that even if you had a difficult childhood yourself, you could still change things this time around for your children. It's never too late. However, even if you didn't have a positive influence growing up, nothing stops you from becoming the influence you so desperately wanted as a child. You can always make a difference and prevent a negative cycle.

The stories listed in this book weren't meant to make you feel good or bad about your own journey or to create comparisons between your childhood and that of others. Instead, I hoped to inspire parents and caregivers to be the best version of themselves, to follow their goals and dreams, not only for themselves but for their children.

Happy parents will find it easier to provide a happy childhood for their children. Determined parents will find it easier to raise determined children. Kind parents will find it easier to raise kind children. Strong parents will find it easier to raise strong children. Your children will grow up to reflect on the experiences they had with you from the very moment they were born, so be very mindful of what type of person and parent you are modeling while raising your children.

Thus, if you have a dream, go after it. Don't limit your efforts, even after parenthood. Chase it. Make it happen. Or, at the very least, try your best. If you have hobbies, keep them. They make who you are, and it's crucial that you don't abandon those particular traits that are special to you. Let your child watch you be who you truly are in your most distinctive and truthful form. We all have a story to tell. It's your story. You are the creator of your life, and you help your children create their own paths whether you intend to or not. Become the person you want to be in front of your children and watch the magic that happens.

ABOUT THE AUTHOR

Dar Batrowny is a child development specialist and the author of a step-by-step motivational book for moms pursuing their dreams entitled *The Power of Moms with Dreams,* a developmental children's series entitled *The Art of Early Learning Series, The Early Ed Series,* as well as many other books. She is the founder of the Maxi Mom Success System and World Child Development Day. She and her husband enjoy spending time in the New York State Finger Lakes Region and the Delmarva Coast. Dar loves spending time with her family. She loves educating and inspiring others to succeed and to live the life of their dreams.

Learn more about Dar's books at https://www.amazon.com/author/dabatrowny.

Learn more about the Maxi Mom Success System, Dar's books, success acceleration course, and gratitude coins at https://beAmastermom.com.

Learn more about child development and her children's books at http://www.darbatrowny.com/ and http://liftAchild.com.

END

www.ingramcontent.com/pod-product-compliance
Lightning Source LLC
LaVergne TN
LVHW051505070426
835507LV00022B/2927